Developmentally Appropriate Practice

SUE BREDEKAMP, *Editor*

D1299497

National Association for the Education of Young Children
1834 Connecticut Avenue, N.W., Washington, DC 20009-5786

Copies of *Developmentally Appropriate Practice* can be purchased from NAEYC, 1834 Connecticut Avenue, N.W., Washington, DC 20009-5786

Library of Congress Catalog Card Number: 86-063034

ISBN Catalog Number: 0-935989-04-8

NAEYC #224

Printed in the United States of America.

Contents

Preface

With the proliferation of programs for young children and the introduction of large numbers of infants and toddlers into group care, early childhood professionals have become increasingly concerned about the quality of care and education provided. Improving the quality of professional practice in programs for young children is one of the main goals of NAEYC and the focus of most of our services. Recently, our most ambitious initiative directed toward that goal was to launch a national, voluntary accreditation system for early childhood centers and schools—the National Academy of Early Childhood Programs.

It was during the development of NAEYC's accreditation Criteria that the need for a clearer definition of *developmentally appropriate practice* first arose. Many of the Criteria refer to "developmentally appropriate activities ... materials ... or expectations." Without further information, these Criteria are subject to varying interpretations. Now that the accreditation system is operating, it has become even more important to have clear descriptions of the meaning of key terms and no concept is more key to defining quality than "developmental appropriateness."

As with so many things, this book represents an in-depth process of development that still continues. Because NAEYC defines *early childhood* as birth through age 8, a generic statement of developmentally appropriate practice across that age span was first developed (Part 1). It was clear from the outset, however, that more succinct statements of appropriate practice for specific age groups were needed. The first statements to be developed were those for which the greatest need had been expressed. Included as Part 4 of this book is a statement of developmentally appropriate practice in programs for 4- and 5-year-olds. This statement is in response to several factors, foremost of which is the concern that many kindergartens and even prekindergartens are becoming watered-down first grades, with too much emphasis on teacher-directed instruction in narrowly defined academic skills.

Also included in this book are statements defining developmentally appropriate care for infants and toddlers. With increasing numbers of children younger than 3 being cared for outside their homes, a major concern is that these very vulnerable human beings get the best possible care during those first, critical years of development. Of particular concern are the important dimensions of social and emotional development that lead to a healthy, well-adjusted sense of self. Part 2 of this volume is a joint publication of NAEYC and the National Center for Clinical Infant Programs. It describes how infants and toddlers develop and includes examples and implications for appropriate care. The implications are further delineated in Part 3 of this book which provides succinct descriptions of both appropriate and inappropriate practices in working with infants and toddlers in group settings. Inappropriate practice is described because people often learn what to do by learning what *not* to do. Sensitive readers will soon see that the younger children are, the more inappropriate practices appear neglectful or border on abusive.

Defining appropriate practice for 4- and 5-year-olds and for infants and toddlers was identified as the most pressing need initially and so this book addresses those age groups most clearly. But development continues, and a second edition of this book will clearly describe appropriate practice across the full age span, birth through 8.

The concept of developmentally appropriate practice can be summarized, to coin Hunt's phrase, as a problem of the match. What is perfectly acceptable for one age group is inappropriate for another because it does not match the child's developmental level. Just as acceptable elementary school practice is often inappropriate for preschoolers, many common preschool practices are inappropriate for toddlers. We shudder at those who would teach 4-year-olds like fourth graders, but we must also shake our heads when 18-month-olds are expected to function like 4-year-olds.

Development is a truly fascinating and wonderful phenomenon. It is not something to be accelerated or skipped. One period of childhood or aspect of development is not better or more important than another; each has its own tasks to accomplish. The descriptions of developmentally appropriate practice in this book are intended to help adults who work with young children provide the best quality care and education for children so that they in turn may develop to their fullest potential.

PART I

NAEYC Position Statement on Developmentally Appropriate Practice in Early Childhood Programs Serving Children From Birth Through Age 8

Introduction

The quality of our nation's educational system has come under intense public scrutiny in the 1980s. While much of the attention has been directed at secondary and postsecondary education, the field of early childhood education must also examine its practices in light of current knowledge of child development and learning.

The purpose of this paper is to describe developmentally appropriate practice in early childhood programs for administrators, teachers, parents, policy makers, and others who make decisions about the care and education of young children. An early childhood program is any part-day or full-day group program in a center, school, or other facility, that serves children from birth through age 8. Early childhood programs include child care centers, private and public preschools, kindergartens, and primary grade schools.

Rationale

In recent years, a trend toward increased emphasis on formal instruction in academic skills has emerged in early childhood programs. This trend toward formal academic instruction for younger children is based on misconceptions about early learning (Elkind, 1986). Despite the trend among some educators to formalize instruction, there has been no comparable evidence of change in what young children need for optimal development or how they learn. In fact, a growing body of research has emerged recently affirming that children learn most effectively through a concrete, play-oriented approach to early childhood education.

In addition to an increased emphasis on academics, early childhood programs have experienced other changes. The number of progams has increased in response to the growing demand for out-of-home care and education during the early years. Some characteristics of early childhood programs have also changed in the last few years. For example, children are now enrolled in programs at younger ages, many from infancy. The length of the program day for all ages of children has been extended in response to the need for extended hours of care for employed families. Similarly, program sponsorship has become more diverse. The public schools are playing a larger role in providing prekindergarten programs or before- and after-school child care. Corporate America is also becoming a more visible sponsor of child care programs.

Programs have changed in response to social, economic, and political forces; however, these changes have not always taken into account the basic developmental needs of young children, which have remained constant. The trend toward early academics, for example, is antithetical to what we know about how young children learn. Programs should be tailored to meet the needs of children, rather than expecting children to adjust to the demands of a specific program.

Position Statement

The National Association for the Education of Young Children (NAEYC) believes that a high quality early childhood program provides a safe and nurturing environment that promotes the physical, social, emotional, and cognitive development of young children while responding to the needs of families. Although the quality of an early childhood program may be affected by many factors, a major determinant of program quality is the extent to which knowledge of child development is applied in program practices—the degree to which

The curriculum and adults' interaction are responsive to individual differences in ability and interests.

the program is *developmentally appropriate.* NAEYC believes that high quality, developmentally appropriate programs should be available to all children and their families.

In this position paper, the concept of *developmental appropriateness* will first be defined. Then guidelines will be presented describing how developmental appropriateness can be applied to four components of early childhood programs: curriculum; adult-child interactions; relations between the home and program; and developmental evaluation of children. The statement concludes with a discussion of major policy implications and recommendations. These guidelines are designed to be used in conjunction with NAEYC's Criteria for High Quality Early Childhood Programs, the standards for accreditation by the National Academy of Early Childhood Programs (NAEYC, 1984).

Definition of developmental appropriateness

The concept of *developmental appropriateness* has two dimensions: age appropriateness and individual appropriateness.

1. **Age appropriateness.** Human development research indicates that there are universal, predictable sequences of growth and change that occur in children during the first 9 years of life. These predictable changes occur in all domains of development—physical, emotional, social, and cognitive. Knowledge of typical development of children within the age span served by the program provides a framework from which teachers prepare the learning environment and plan appropriate experiences.

2. **Individual appropriateness.** Each child is a unique person with an individual pattern and timing of growth, as well as individual personality, learning style, and family background. Both the curriculum and adults' interactions with children should be responsive to individual differences. Learning in young children is the result of interaction between the child's thoughts and experiences with materials, ideas, and people. These experiences should match the child's developing abilities, while also challenging the child's interest and understanding.

Teachers can use child development knowledge to identify the range of appropriate behaviors, activities, and materials for a specific age group. This knowledge is used in conjunction with understanding about individual children's growth patterns, strengths, interests, and experiences to design the most appropriate learning environment. Although the content of the curriculum is determined by many factors such as tradition, the subject matter of the disciplines, social or cultural values, and parental desires, for the content and teaching strategies to be develomentally appropriate they must be age appropriate and individually appropriate.

Children's play is a primary vehicle for and indicator of their mental growth. Play enables children to progress along the developmental sequence from the sensorimotor intelligence of infancy to preoperational thought in the preschool years to the concrete operational thinking exhibited by primary children (Fein, 1979; Fromberg, 1986; Piaget, 1952; Sponseller, 1982). In addition to its role in cognitive development, play also serves important functions in children's physical, emotional, and social development (Herron & Sutton-Smith, 1974). Therefore, child-initiated, child-directed, teacher-supported play is an essential component of developmentally appropriate practice (Fein & Rivkin, 1986).

Guidelines for Developmentally Appropriate Practice

I. Curriculum

A developmentally appropriate curriculum for young children is planned to be appropriate for the age span of the children within the group and is implemented with attention to the different needs, interests, and developmental levels of those individual children.

A. Developmentally appropriate curriculum provides for all areas of a child's development: physical, emotional, social, and cognitive through an integrated approach (Almy, 1975; Biber, 1984; Elkind, 1986; Forman & Kuschner, 1983; Kline, 1985; Skeen, Garner, & Cartwright, 1984; Spodek, 1985).

Realistic curriculum goals for children should address all of these areas in age-appropriate ways. Children's learning does not occur in narrowly defined subject areas; their development and learning are integrated. Any activity that stimulates one dimension of development and learning affects other dimensions as well.

B. Appropriate curriculum planning is based on teachers' observations and recordings of each child's special interests and developmental progress (Almy, 1975; Biber, 1984; Cohen, Stern, & Balaban, 1983; Goodman & Goodman, 1982).

Realistic curriculum goals and plans are based on regular assessment of individual needs, strengths, and interests. Curriculum is based on both age-appropriate and individually appropriate information. For example, individual children's family/cultural backgrounds—such as expressive styles, ways of interacting, play, and games—are used to broaden the curriculum for all children.

C. Curriculum planning emphasizes learning as an interactive process. Teachers prepare the environment for children to learn through active exploration and interaction with adults, other children, and materials (Biber, 1984; Fein, 1979; Forman & Kuschner, 1983; Fromberg, 1986; Goffin & Tull, 1985; Griffin, 1982; Kamii, 1985; Lay-Dopyera & Dopyera, 1986; Powell, 1986; Sponseller, 1982).

The process of interacting with materials and people results in learning. Finished products or "correct" solutions that conform to adult standards are not very accurate criteria for judging whether learning has occurred. Much of young children's learning takes place when they direct their own play activities. During play, children feel successful when they engage in a task they have defined for themselves, such as finding their way through an obstacle course with a friend or pouring water into and out of various containers. Such learning should not be inhibited by adult-established concepts of completion, achievement, and failure. Activities should be designed to concentrate on furthering emerging skills through creative activity and intense involvement.

D. Learning activities and materials should be concrete, real, and relevant to the lives of young children (Almy, 1975; Biber, 1984; Evans, 1984; Forman & Kuschner, 1983; Hawkins, 1970; Hirsch, 1984; Holt, 1979; Kamii, 1985; Kline, 1985; Piaget, 1972; Schickedanz, 1986; Seefeldt, 1986; Smith, 1985; Weber, 1984).

Children need years of play with real objects and events before they are able to understand the meaning of symbols such as letters and numbers. Learning takes place as young children touch, manipulate, and experiment with things and interact with people. Throughout early childhood, children's concepts and language gradually develop to enable them to understand more abstract or symbolic information. Pictures and stories should be used frequently to build upon children's real experiences.

Workbooks, worksheets, coloring books, and adult-made models of art products for children to copy are *not* appropriate for young children, especially those younger than 6. Children older than 5 show increasing abilities to learn through written exercises, oral presentations, and other adult-directed teaching strategies.

Child-initiated, child-directed, teacher-supported play is an essential component of developmentally appropriate practice.

However, the child's active participation in self-directed play with concrete, real-life experiences continues to be a key to motivated, meaningful learning in kindergarten and the primary grades.

Basic learning materials and activities for an appropriate curriculum include sand, water, clay, and accessories to use with them; table, unit, and hollow blocks; puzzles with varying numbers of pieces; many types of games; a variety of small manipulative toys; dramatic play props such as those for housekeeping and transportation; a variety of science investigation equipment and items to explore; a changing selection of appropriate and aesthetically pleasing books and recordings; supplies of paper, water-based paint, and markers, and other materials for creative expression; large muscle equipment; field trips; classroom responsibilities, such as helping with routines; and positive interactions and problem-solving opportunities with other children and adults.

E. Programs provide for a wider range of developmental interests and abilities than the chronological age range of the group would suggest. Adults are prepared to meet the needs of children who exhibit unusual interests and skills outside the normal developmental range (Kitano, 1982; Languis, Sanders, & Tipps, 1980; Schickedanz, Schickedanz, & Forsyth, 1982; Souweine, Crimmins, & Mazel, 1981; Uphoff & Gilmore, 1985).

Activities and equipment should be provided for a chronological age range which in many cases is at least 12 months. However, the normal developmental age range in any group may be as much as 2 years. Some mainstreamed situations will demand a wider range of expectations. When the developmental age range of a group is more than 18 months, the need increases for a large variety of furnishings, equipment, and teaching strategies. The complexity of materials should also reflect the age span of the group. For example, a group that includes 3-, 4-, and 5-year-olds would need books of varying length and complexity; puzzles with varying numbers and sizes of pieces; games that require a range of skills and abilities to follow rules; and other diverse materials, teaching methods, and room arrangements.

F. Teachers provide a variety of activities and materials; teachers increase the difficulty, complexity, and challenge of an activity as children are involved with it and as children develop understanding and skills (Davidson, 1985; Ferreiro & Teberosky, 1982; Forman & Kaden, 1986; Gerber, 1982; Gilbert, 1981; Gonzalez-Mena & Eyer, 1980; Greenberg, 1976; Hill, 1979; Hirsch, 1984; Holt, 1979; Honig, 1980, 1981; Kamii, 1982, 1985; Kamii & DeVries, 1980; Lasky & Mukerji, 1980; McDonald, 1979; National Institute of Education, 1984; Schickedanz, 1986; Smith, 1982; Smith, 1983; Sparling, 1984; Stewart, 1982; Veach, 1977; Willert & Kamii, 1985; Willis & Ricciuti, 1975).

As children work with materials or activities, teachers listen, observe, and interpret children's behavior. Teachers can then facilitate children's involvement and learning by asking questions, making suggestions, or adding more complex materials or ideas to a situation. During a program year, as well as from one year to another, activities and environments

Learning activities and materials should be concrete, real, and relevant to the lives of young children.

for children should change in arrangement and inventory, and special events should also be planned. Examples of developmentally appropriate learning activities for various age groups follow.

1. Infants and toddlers

Infants and toddlers learn by experiencing the environment through their senses (seeing, hearing, tasting, smelling, and feeling), by physically moving around, and through social interaction. Nonmobile infants absorb and organize a great deal of information about the world around them, so adults talk and sing with them about what is happening and bring them objects to observe and manipulate. At times adults carry nonmobile infants around the environment to show them interesting events and people. Mobile infants and toddlers increasingly use toys, language, and other learning materials in their play.

Adults play a vital socialization role with infants and toddlers. Warm, positive relationships with adults help infants develop a sense of trust in the world and feelings of competence. These interactions are critical for the development of the children's healthy self-esteem. The trusted adult becomes the secure base from which the mobile infant or toddler explores the environment.

Important independence skills are being acquired during these years, including personal care such as toileting, feeding, and dressing. The most appropriate teaching technique for this age group is to give ample opportunities for the children to use self-initiated repetition to practice newly acquired skills and to experience feelings of autonomy and success. Infants will bat at, grasp, bang, or drop their toys. Patience is essential as a toddler struggles to put on a sweater. Imitation, hiding, and naming games are also important for learning at this age. Realistic toys will enable children to engage in increasingly complex types of play.

Two-year-olds are learning to produce language rapidly. They need simple books, pictures, puzzles, and music, and time and space for active play such as jumping, running, and dancing. Toddlers are acquiring

5

Infants and toddlers learn by experiencing the environment through their senses.

social skills, but in groups there should be several of the same toy because egocentric toddlers are not yet able to understand the concept of sharing.

2. Three-, 4-, and 5-year-olds

Curriculum for 3-year-olds should emphasize language, activity, and movement, with major emphasis on large muscle activity. Appropriate activities include dramatic play, wheel toys and climbers, puzzles and blocks, and opportunities to talk and listen to simple stories.

Four-year-olds enjoy a greater variety of experiences and more small motor activities like scissors, art, manipulatives, and cooking. They are more able to concentrate and remember as well as recognize objects by shape, color, or size. Four-year-olds are developing basic math concepts and problem-solving skills.

Some 4-year-olds and most 5-year-olds combine ideas into more complex relations (for example, number concepts such as one-to-one correspondence) and have growing memory capacity and fine motor physical skills. Some 4-year-olds and most 5's display a growing interest in the functional aspects of written language, such as recognizing meaningful words and trying to write their own names. Activities designed solely to teach the alphabet, phonics, and penmanship are much less appropriate for this age group than providing a print-rich environment that stimulates the development of language and literacy skills in a meaningful context.

Curriculum for 4's and 5's can expand beyond the child's immediate experience of self, home, and family to include special events and trips. Five-year-olds are developing interest in community and the world outside their own. They also use motor skills well, even daringly, and show increasing ability to pay attention for longer times and in larger groups if the topic is meaningful.

3. Six-, 7-, and 8-year-olds

Six-year-olds are active and demonstrate considerable verbal ability; they are becoming interested in games and rules and develop concepts and problem-solving skills from these experiences. Most 6-year-olds and many 7- and 8-year-olds may be more mature mentally than physically. Therefore, hands-on activity and experimentation is more appropriate for this age group than fatiguing mechanical seatwork.

Seven-year-olds seem to need time to catch up and practice with many newly acquired physical and cognitive skills. They become increasingly able to reason, to listen to others, and to show social give-and-take.

Eight-year-olds combine great curiosity with increased social interest. Now they are able to learn about other, more distant peoples. During first, second, and third grade, children can learn from the symbolic experiences of reading books and listening to stories; however, their understanding of what they read is based on their ability to relate the written word to their own experience. Primary grade children also learn to communicate through written language, dictating or writing stories about their own experiences or fantasies. The same is true of the development of number concepts. Children's mathematical concepts develop from their own thinking during games and real-life experiences that involve quantification, such as cooking or carpentry.

Teachers increase the difficulty, complexity, and challenge of an activity as children are involved with it and as children develop understanding and skills.

Marietta Lynch

G. **Adults provide opportunities for children to choose from among a variety of activities, materials, and equipment; and time to explore through active involvement. Adults facilitate children's engagement with materials and activities and extend the child's learning by asking questions or making suggestions that stimulate children's thinking** (Elkind, 1986; Forman & Kuschner, 1983; Goffin & Tull, 1985; Kamii & Lee-Katz, 1979; Lay-Dopyera & Dopyera, 1986; Sackoff & Hart, 1984; Skeen, Garner, & Cartwright, 1984; Sparling, 1984).

Children of all ages need uninterrupted periods of time to become involved, investigate, select, and persist at activities. The teacher's role in child-chosen activity is to prepare the environment with stimulating, challenging activity choices and then to facilitate children's engagement. In developmentally appropriate programs, adults:

1. provide a rich variety of activities and materials from which to choose.

    Such variety increases the likelihood of a child's prolonged or satisfied attention and increases independence and opportunity for making decisions.

2. offer children the choice to participate in a small group or in a solitary activity.

3. assist and guide children who are not yet able to use easily and enjoy child-choice activity periods.

4. provide opportunities for child-initiated, child-directed practice of skills as a self-chosen activity.

    Children need opportunities to repeat acquired skills to fully assimilate their learning. Repetition that is initiated and directed by the child, not adult-directed drill and practice, is most valuable for assimilation.

H. **Multicultural and nonsexist experiences, materials, and equipment should be provided for children of all ages** (Ramsey, 1979, 1980, 1982; Saracho & Spodek, 1983; Sprung, 1978).

Providing a wide variety of multicultural, nonstereotyping materials and activities helps ensure the individual appropriateness of the curriculum and also

1. enhances each child's self-concept and esteem,

2. supports the integrity of the child's family,

3. enhances the child's learning processes in both the home and the early childhood program by strengthening ties,

4. extends experiences of children and their families to include knowledge of the ways of others, especially those who share the community, and

5. enriches the lives of all participants with respectful acceptance and appreciation of differences and similarities among them.

Multicultural experiences should not be limited to a celebration of holidays and should include foods, music, families, shelter, and other aspects common to all cultures.

Multicultural experiences should not be limited to a celebration of holidays and should include foods, music, families, shelter, and other aspects common to all cultures.

Nya Kwiawon Taryor

I. Adults provide a balance of rest and active movement for children throughout the program day (Cratty, 1982; Curtis, 1986; Hendrick, 1986; Stewart, 1982; Willis & Ricciuti, 1975).

For infants and toddlers, naps and quiet activities such as listening to rhymes and music provide periodic rest from the intense physical exploration that is characteristic of this age group. Two-year-olds, and many 3's, will need morning and/or afternoon naps, and should also have periods of carefully planned transition to quieting-down or rousing, especially before and after eating and sleeping. Children at about 2½- to 3-years-old become able to maintain brief interest in occasional small-group, teacher-conducted activities, and may enjoy quiet stories, music, and fingerplays together between periods of intense activity. Most 4's and many 5's still need naps, especially if their waking days are very long as they are in some child care situations. Children at this age need planned alternations of active and quiet activities and are usually willing to participate in brief, interesting, small-group activities. Older children continue to need alternating periods of active and quiet activity throughout the day, beyond traditionally provided recess.

The pace of the program day will vary depending on the length of time children are present, but children should never be rushed and schedules should be flexible enough to take advantage of impromptu experiences. The balance between active and quiet activity should be maintained throughout the day by alternating activities.

J. Outdoor experiences should be provided for children of all ages (Cratty, 1982; Curtis, 1986; Frost & Klein, 1979).

Because their physical development is occurring so rapidly, young children through age 8 need daily outdoor experiences to practice large muscle skills, learn about outdoor environments, and experience freedom not always possible indoors. Outdoor time is an integral part of the curriculum and requires planning; it is not simply a time for children to release pent-up energy.

Children should never be rushed and schedules should be flexible enough to take advantage of impromptu experiences. The balance between active and quiet activity should be maintained throughout the day.

Steve Herzog

respond appropriately to infants' vocalizations, manipulation of objects, and movement, as these are the ways infants communicate. Adults hold and touch infants frequently; talk and sing to infants in a soothing, friendly voice; smile and maintain eye contact with infants. For toddlers and 2-year-olds, adults remain close by, giving attention and physical comfort as needed. Adults repeat children's words, paraphrase, or use synonyms or actions to help assure toddlers that they are understood. As children get older, adult responses are characterized by less physical communication and more verbal responsiveness, although immediacy is still important. Positive responses such as smiles and interest, and concentrated attention on children's activity, are important. Adults move quietly and circulate among individuals in groups to communicate with children in a friendly and relaxed manner.

II. Adult-Child Interaction

The developmental appropriateness of an early childhood program is most apparent in the interactions between adults and children. Developmentally appropriate interactions are based on adults' knowledge and expectations of age-appropriate behavior in children balanced by adults' awareness of individual differences among children.

A. Adults respond quickly and directly to children's needs, desires, and messages and adapt their responses to children's differing styles and abilities (Bell & Ainsworth, 1972; Erikson, 1950; Genishi, 1986; Greenspan & Greenspan, 1985; Honig, 1980, 1981; Lozoff, Brillenham, Trause, Kennell, & Klaus, 1977; Shure & Spivak, 1978; Smith & Davis, 1976).

Appropriate responses vary with the age of the child. Adults should respond immediately to infants' cries of distress. The response should be warm and soothing as the adult identifies the child's needs. Adults should also

Subjects & Predicates

The developmental appropriateness of an early childhood program is most apparent in the interactions between adults and children.

9

From infancy through the primary grades, adult communication with children is facilitated by sitting low or kneeling, and making eye contact. With all age groups, adults should also be aware of the powerful influence of modeling and other nonverbal communication; adults' actions should be compatible with their verbal messages and confirm that children understand their messages.

B. **Adults provide many varied opportunities for children to communicate** (Cazden, 1981; Genishi, 1986; Gordon, 1970, 1975; Greenspan & Greenspan, 1985; Lay-Dopyera & Dopyera, 1986; McAfee, 1985; Schachter & Strage, 1982; Schickendanz, 1986).

Children acquire communication skills through hearing and using language, and as adults listen and respond to what children say. Communication skills grow out of the desire to use language to express needs, insights, and excitement, and to solve problems. Children do not learn language, or any other concepts, by being quiet and listening to a lecture from an adult. Listening experiences—when there is something meaningful to listen to such as a story or poetry—can enrich language learning. Most language interaction with infants and toddlers is on an individual basis, although occasionally a group of two or three children may gather to hear an absorbing story. Throughout the preschool years, individual abilities to sit and pay attention will vary considerably, but time periods are short and groups should be small. During kindergarten and the primary grades, children can listen to directions or stories for longer periods of time (gradually expanding as children get older). Individual and small group interactions are still the most effective because children have the opportunity for two-way communication with adults and other children. Total group instructional techniques are *not* as effective in facilitating the development of communication skills and other learning in young children.

Equally important are opportunities for children to engage in two-way communication with others. Infants use crying and body movements to communicate. Adult responses to this communication, including the use of soothing language and descriptions of what is happening, build the foundation for children's

ability to use language and their ability to feel good about themselves. Children rapidly expand their ability to understand language in their early years, and from about the age of 2, children can engage in increasingly interesting and lengthy conversations with adults and other children. These one-on-one exchanges are critical throughout the early years. Children's questions, and their responses to questions, particularly open-ended questions, provide valuable information about the individual's level of thinking.

C. **Adults facilitate a child's successful completion of tasks by providing support, focused attention, physical proximity, and verbal encouragement. Adults recognize that children learn from trial and error and that children's misconceptions reflect their developing thoughts** (Cohen, Stern, & Balaban, 1983; Elkind, 1986; Gottfried, 1983; Kamii, 1985; Piaget, 1950; Veach, 1977; Wallinga & Sweaney, 1985; Wellman, 1982; Zavitkovsky, Baker, Berlfein, & Almy, 1986).

Real successes are important incentives for people of all ages to continue learning and maintain motivation. Children learn from their own mistakes. Adults can examine the problem with the child and, if appropriate, encourage the child to try again or to find alternatives. Teachers plan many open-ended activities that have more than one right answer, and value the unique responses of individual children.

D. **Teachers are alert to signs of undue stress in children's behavior, and aware of appropriate stress-reducing activities and techniques** (Dreikurs, Grunwald, & Pepper, 1982; Elkind, 1986; Gazda, 1973; Honig, 1986; McCracken, 1986; Warren, 1977).

Formal, inappropriate instructional techniques are a source of stress for young children. When children exhibit stress-related behavior, teachers should examine the program to ensure that expectations are appropriate and not placing excessive demands on children.

When children experience stress from other sources, adults can find ways to reduce or eliminate the problem, or help children cope with it. Appropriate adult behaviors may include cuddling and soothing a crying infant; offering a toddler a favorite toy; providing books, water play, body movement, music, and quiet times for older children; and physically comforting and listening to the concerns of a child of any age who is in distress. Children's responses to stress are as individual as their learning styles. An understanding adult who is sensitive to individual children's reactions is the key to providing appropriate comfort.

E. Adults facilitate the development of self-esteem by expressing respect, acceptance, and comfort for children, regardless of the child's behavior (Coppersmith, 1975; Gordon, 1970, 1975; Greenspan & Greenspan, 1985; Kobak, 1979; Kuczynski, 1983; Lickona, 1983; Moore, 1982; Mussen & Eisenberg-Bert, 1977; Riley, 1984; Rubin & Everett, 1982; Smith & Davis, 1976; Stone, 1978).

Understanding behavior that is not unusual for young children, such as messiness, interest in body parts and genital differences, crying and resistance, aggression, and later infraction of rules and truth, is the basis for appropriate guidance of young children. Developmentally appropriate guidance demonstrates respect for children. It helps them understand and grow, and is directed toward helping children develop self-control and the ability to make better decisions in the future.

Adult behaviors that are *never* acceptable toward children include: screaming in anger; neglect; inflicting physical or emotional pain; criticism of a child's person or family by ridiculing, blaming, teasing, insulting, name-calling, threatening, or using frightening or humiliating punishment. Adults should not laugh at children's behavior, nor discuss it among themselves in the presence of children.

F. Adults facilitate the development of self-control in children (Asher, Renshaw, & Hymel, 1982; Hoffman, 1975; Honig, 1985; Kopp, 1982; Lytton, 1979; Miller, 1984; Moore, 1982; Read, Gardner, & Mahler, 1986; Rogers & Ross, 1986; Schaffer, 1984; Stone, 1978; Wolfgang & Glickman, 1980; Yarrow, Scott, & Waxler, 1973; Yarrow & Waxler, 1976).

Children learn self-control when adults treat

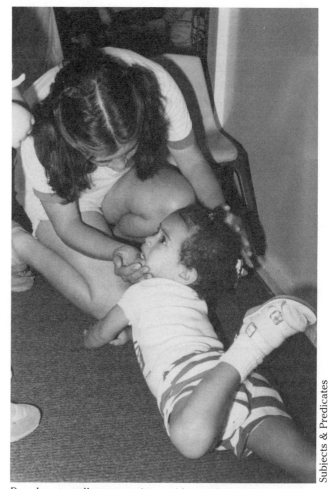

Subjects & Predicates

Developmentally appropriate guidance demonstrates respect for children. It helps them understand and grow and is directed toward helping children develop self-control and the ability to make better decisions in the future.

them with dignity and use discipline techniques such as

1. guiding children by setting clear, consistent, fair limits for classroom behavior; or in the case of older children, helping them to set their own limits;

2. valuing mistakes as learning opportunities;

3. redirecting children to more acceptable behavior or activity;

4. listening when children talk about their feelings and frustrations;

5. guiding children to resolve conflicts and modeling skills that help children to solve their own problems; and

6. patiently reminding children of rules and their rationale as needed.

11

G. Adults are responsible for all children under their supervision at all times and plan for increasing independence as children acquire skills (Stewart, 1982; Veach, 1977).

Adults must constantly and closely supervise and attend every child younger than the age of 3. They must be close enough to touch infants when awake, catch a climbing toddler before she hits the ground, be aware of every move of a 2-year-old, and be close enough to offer another toy when 2-year-olds have difficulty sharing. Adults must be responsible for 3- to 5-year-old children at all times, in an environment sufficiently open to permit it. Children older than 5 may be deemed, on individual bases, mature enough to leave the classroom or run independent errands within a building. This should happen only with the adult's permission and specific knowledge.

Children in all early childhood settings must be protected from unauthorized (by the guardian/family) adults and older children. Parents should be welcome visitors in the program, but provisions should be made for limited access to buildings, careful and close supervision of outdoor play areas, and policies which demand that visiting adults check with the administrative office before entering the children's areas. Constant adult vigilance is required with children birth through age 8 years. Young children should not be given the burden of protecting themselves from adults.

III. Relations Between the Home and Program

To achieve individually appropriate programs for young children, early childhood teachers must work in partnership with families and communicate regularly with children's parents.

A. Parents have both the right and the responsibility to share in decisions about their children's care and education. Parents should be encouraged to observe and participate. Teachers are responsible for establishing and maintaining frequent contacts with families (Brazelton, 1984; Croft, 1979; Dittmann, 1984; Honig, 1982; Katz, 1980; Lightfoot, 1978; Moore, 1982; Weissbourd, 1981).

During early childhood, children are largely dependent on their families for identity, security, care, and a general sense of well-being. Communication between families and teachers helps build mutual understanding and guidance, and provides greater consistency for children. Joint planning between families and teachers facilitates major socialization processes, such as toilet learning, developing peer relationships, and entering school.

B. Teachers share child development knowledge, insights, and resources as part of regular communication and conferences with family members (Brazelton, 1984; Croft, 1979; Dittmann, 1984; Lightfoot, 1978).

Mutual sharing of information and insights about the individual child's needs and developmental strides help both the family and the program. Regular communication and understanding about child development form a basis for mutual problem solving about concerns regarding behavior and growth. Teachers seek information from parents about individual children. Teachers promote mutual respect by recognizing and acknowledging different points of view to help minimize confusion for children.

C. Teachers, parents, agencies, programs, and consultants who may have educational responsibility for the child at different times should, with family participation, share developmental information about children as they pass from one level or program to another (Lightfoot, 1978; Meisels, 1985; Read, Gardner, & Mahler, 1986; Ziegler, 1985).

Continuity of educational experience is critical to supporting development. Such continuity results from communication both horizontally, as children change programs within a given year, and vertically, as children move on to other settings.

IV. Developmental Evaluation of Children

Assessment of individual children's development and learning is essential for planning and implementing developmentally appropriate programs, but should be used with caution to prevent discrimination against individuals and to ensure accuracy. Accurate testing can only be achieved with reliable, valid instruments and such instruments developed for use with young children are extremely rare. In the absence of valid instruments, testing is not valuable. Therefore, assessment of young children should rely heavily on the results of observations of their development and descriptive data.

A. Decisions that have a major impact on children such as enrollment, retention, or placement are not made on the basis of a single developmental assessment or screening device but consider other relevant information, particularly observations by teachers and parents. Developmental assessment of children's progress and achievements is used to adapt curriculum to match the developmental needs of children, to communicate with the child's family, and to evaluate the program's effectiveness (Cohen, Stern, & Balaban, 1983; Goodman & Goodman, 1982; Meisels, 1985; Standards for Educational and Psychological Testing, 1985; Uphoff & Gilmore, 1985).

Children acquire knowledge about the physical and social worlds in which they live through playful interaction with objects and people.

Marietta Lynch

Scores on psychometric tests that measure narrowly defined academic skills should never be the sole criterion for recommending enrollment or retention in a program, or placement in special or remedial classes. Likewise, assessment of children should be used to evaluate the effectiveness of the curriculum, but the performance of children on standardized tests should not determine curriculum decisions.

B. Developmental assessments and observations are used to identify children who have special needs and/or who are at risk and to plan appropriate curriculum for them (Meisels, 1985).

This information is used to provide appropriate programming for these children and may be used in making professional referrals to families.

C. Developmental expectations based on standardized measurements and norms should compare any child or group of children only to normative information that is not only age-matched, but also gender-, culture-, and socioeconomically appropriate (Meisels, 1985; Standards for Educational and Psychological Testing, 1985; Uphoff & Gilmore, 1985).

The validity of comparative data analysis is questionable in the absence of such considerations.

D. In public schools, there should be a developmentally appropriate placement for every child of legal entry age.

No public school program should deny access to children of legal entry age on the basis of lack of maturational "readiness." For example, a kindergarten program that denies access to many 5-year-olds is not meeting the needs of its clients. Curriculum should be planned for the developmental levels of children and emphasize individual planning to address a wide range of developmental levels in a single classroom. It is the responsibility of the educational system to adjust to the developmental needs and levels of the children it serves; children should not be expected to adapt to an inappropriate system.

Policies Essential for Achieving Developmentally Appropriate Early Childhood Programs

The following policies are essential to implement NAEYC's Guidelines for Developmentally Appropriate Practice in Early Childhood Programs Serving Children From Birth Through Age 8. NAEYC strongly recommends that policy-making groups at the state and local levels consider the following when implementing early childhood programs.

A. Early childhood teachers should have college-level specialized preparation in early childhood education/child development. Teachers in early childhood programs, regardless of credentialed status, should be encouraged and supported to obtain and maintain current knowledge of child development and its application to early childhood educational practice (Almy, 1982; Feeney & Chun, 1985; NAEYC, 1982, 1985; Ruopp, Travers, Glantz, & Coelen, 1979).

Teachers must be knowledgeable about child development before they can implement a program based on child development principles. Implementing a developmentally appropriate program also requires preparation that is specifically designed for teaching young children through an individualized, concrete, experiential approach. Such preparation includes a foundation in theory and research of child development from birth through age 8, developmentally appropriate instructional methods, and field experiences.

B. Early childhood teachers should have practical experience teaching the age group. Therefore, regardless of credentialed status, teachers who have not previously taught young children should have supervised experience with young children before they can be in charge of a group (NAEYC, 1982, 1984).

C. Implementation of developmentally appropriate early childhood programs requires limiting the size of the group and providing sufficient numbers of adults to provide individualized and age-appropriate care and education (NAEYC, 1985; Ruopp, Travers, Glantz, & Coelen, 1979).

Even the most well-qualified teacher cannot individualize instruction and adequately supervise too large a group of young children. An acceptable adult-child ratio for 4- and 5-year-olds is 2 adults with no more than 20 children. Younger children require much smaller groups. Group size, and thus ratio of children to adults, should increase gradually through the primary grades.

References

These references include both laboratory and clinical classroom research to document the broad-based literature that forms the foundation for sound practice in early childhood education.

Almy, M. (1975). *The early childhood educator at work.* New York: McGraw-Hill.

Almy, M. (1982). Day care and early childhood education. In E. Zigler & E. Gordon (Eds.), *Daycare: Scientific and social policy issues* (pp. 476–495). Boston: Auburn House.

Asher, S. R., Renshaw, P. D., & Hymel, S. (1982). Peer relations and the development of social skills. In S. G. Moore & C. R. Cooper (Eds.), *The young child: Reviews of research* (Vol. 3, pp. 137–158). Washington, DC: NAEYC.

Bell, S., & Ainsworth, M. D. S. (1972). Infant crying and maternal responsiveness. *Child Development, 43,* 1171–1190.

Biber, B. (1984). *Early education and psychological development.* New Haven: Yale University Press.

Brazelton, T. B. (1984). Cementing family relationships through child care. In L. Dittmann (Ed.), *The infants we care for* (rev. ed.). Washington, DC: NAEYC.

Cazden, C. (Ed.). (1981). *Language in early childhood education* (rev. ed.). Washington, DC: NAEYC.

Cohen, D. H., Stern, V., & Balaban, N. (1983). *Observing and recording the behavior of young children* (3rd ed.). New York: Teachers College Press, Columbia University.

Coopersmith, S. (1975). Building self-esteem in the classroom. In S. Coopersmith (Ed.), *Developing motivation in young children.* San Francisco: Albion.

Cratty, B. (1982). Motor development in early childhood: Critical issues for researchers in the 1980s. In B. Spodek (Ed.), *Handbook of research in early childhood education*. New York: Free Press.

Croft, D. J. (1979). *Parents and teachers: A resource book for home, school, and community relations*. Belmont, CA: Wadsworth.

Curtis, S. (1986). New views on movement development and implications for curriculum in early childhood education. In C. Seefeldt (Ed.), *Early childhood curriculum: A review of current research*. New York: Teachers College Press, Columbia University.

Davidson, L. (1985). Preschool children's tonal knowledge: Antecedents of scale. In J. Boswell (Ed.), *The young child and music: Contemporary principles in child development and music education. Proceedings of the Music in Early Childhood Conference* (pp. 25–40). Reston, VA: Music Educators National Conference.

Dittmann, L. (1984). *The infants we care for*. Washington, DC: NAEYC.

Dreikurs, R., Grunwald, B., & Pepper, S. (1982). *Maintaining sanity in the classroom*. New York: Harper & Row.

Elkind, D. (1986, May). Formal education and early childhood education: An essential difference. *Phi Delta Kappan*, 631–636.

Erikson, E. (1950). *Childhood and society*. New York: Norton.

Evans, E. D. (1984). Children's aesthetics. In L. G. Katz (Ed.), *Current topics in early childhood education* (Vol. 5, pp. 73–104). Norwood, NJ: Ablex.

Feeney, S., & Chun, R. (1985). Research in review. Effective teachers of young children. *Young Children, 41*(1), 47–52.

Fein, G. (1979). Play and the acquisition of symbols. In L. Katz (Ed.), *Current topics in early childhood education* (Vol. 2). Norwood, NJ: Ablex.

Fein, G., & Rivkin, M. (Eds.). (1986). *The young child at play: Reviews of research* (Vol. 4). Washington, DC: NAEYC.

Ferreiro, E., & Teberosky, A. (1982). *Literacy before schooling*. Exeter, NH: Heinemann.

Forman, G., & Kaden, M. (1986). Research on science education in young children. In C. Seefeldt (Ed.), *Early childhood curriculum: A review of current research*. New York: Teachers College Press, Columbia University.

Forman, G., & Kuschner, D. (1983). *The child's construction of knowledge: Piaget for teaching children*. Washington, DC: NAEYC.

Fromberg, D. (1986). Play. In C. Seefeldt (Ed.), *Early childhood curriculum: A review of current research*. New York: Teachers College Press, Columbia University.

Frost, J. L., & Klein, B. L. (1979). *Children's play and playgrounds*. Austin, TX: Playgrounds International.

Gazda, G. M. (1973). *Human relations development: A manual for educators*. Boston: Allyn & Bacon.

Genishi, C. (1986). Acquiring language and communicative competence. In C. Seefeldt (Ed.), *Early childhood curriculum: A review of current research*. New York: Teachers College Press, Columbia University.

Gerber, M. (1982). What is appropriate curriculum for infants and toddlers? In B. Weissbourd & J. Musick (Eds.), *Infants: Their social environments*. Washington, DC: NAEYC.

Gilbert, J. P. (1981). Motoric music skill development in young children: A longitudinal investigation. *Psychology of Music, 9*(1), 21–24.

Goffin, S., & Tull, C. (1985). Problem solving: Encouraging active learning. *Young Children, 40*(3), 28–32.

Gonzales-Mena, J., & Eyer, D. W. (1980). *Infancy and caregiving*. Palo Alto, CA: Mayfield.

Goodman, W., & Goodman, L. (1982). Measuring young children. In B. Spodek (Ed.), *Handbook of research in early childhood education*. New York: Free Press.

Gordon, T. (1970). *Parent effectiveness training*. New York: Wyden.

Gordon, T. (1975). *Teacher effectiveness training*. New York: McKay.

Gottfried, A. (1983). Research in review. Intrinsic motivation in young children. *Young Children, 39*(1), 64–73.

Greenberg, M. (1976). Research in music in early childhood education: A survey with recommendations. *Council for Research in Music Education, 45*, 1–20.

Greenspan, S., & Greenspan, N. T. (1985). *First feelings: Milestones in the emotional development of your baby and child*. New York: Viking.

Griffin, E. F. (1982). *The island of childhood: Education in the special world of nursery school*. Teachers College Press, Columbia University.

Hawkins, D. (1970). Messing about in science. *ESS Reader*. Newton, MA: Education Development Center.

Hendrick, J. (1986). *Total learning: Curriculum for the young child* (2nd ed.). Columbus, OH: Merrill.

Herron, R., & Sutton-Smith, B. (1974). *Child's play*. New York: Wiley.

Hill, D. (1979). *Mud, sand, and water*. Washington, DC: NAEYC.

Hirsch, E. (Ed.). (1984). *The block book*. Washington, DC: NAEYC.

Hoffman, M. L. (1975). Moral internalization, parental power, and the nature of parent-child interaction. *Developmental Psychology, 11*, 228–239.

Holt, B. (1979). *Science with young children*. Washington, DC: NAEYC.

Honig, A. S. (1980). The young child and you—learning together. *Young Children, 35*(4), 2–10.

Honig, A. S. (1981). What are the needs of infants? *Young Children, 37*(1), 3–10.

Honig, A. S. (1982). Parent involvement in early childhood education. In B. Spodek (Ed.), *Handbook of research in early childhood education*. New York: Free Press.

Honig, A. S. (1985). Research in review. Compliance, control, and discipline (Parts 1 & 2). *Young Children, 40*(2) 50–58; *40*(3) 47–52.

Honig, A. S. (1986). Research in review. Stress and coping in children (Parts 1 & 2). *Young Children, 41*(4) 50–63; *41*(5) 47–59.

Kamii, C. (1982). *Number in preschool and kindergarten*. Washington, DC: NAEYC.

Kamii, C. (1985). Leading primary education toward excellence: Beyond worksheets and drill. *Young Children, 40*(6), 3–9.

Kamii, C., & DeVries, R. (1980). *Group games in early education*. Washington, DC: NAEYC.

Kamii, C., & Lee-Katz, L. (1979). Physics in early childhood education: A Piagetian approach. *Young Children, 34*(4), 4–9.

Katz, L. (1980). Mothering and teaching: Some significant distinctions. In L. Katz (Ed.), *Current topics in early childhood education* (Vol. 3, pp. 47–64). Norwood, NJ: Ablex.

Kitano, M. (1982). Young gifted children: Strategies for preschool teachers. *Young Children, 37*(4), 14–24.

Kline, L. W. (1985). *Learning to read, teaching to read*. Newark, DE: LWK Enterprises.

Kobak, D. (1979). Teaching children to care. *Children Today, 8*, 6–7, 34–35.

Kohlberg, L., & Mayer, R. (1972). Development as the aim of education. *Harvard Educational Review, 42*, 449–496.

Kopp, C. B. (1982). Antecedents of self-regulation: A developmental perspective. *Developmental Psychology, 18*, 199–214.

Kuczynski, L. (1983). Reasoning, prohibitions, and motivations for compliance. *Developmental Psychology, 19*, 126–134.

Languis, M., Sanders, T., & Tipps, S. (1980). *Brain and learning: Directions in early childhood education*. Washington, DC: NAEYC.

Lasky, L., & Mukerji, R. (1980). *Art: Basic for young children*. Washington, DC: NAEYC.

Lay-Dopyera, M., & Dopyera, J. (1986). Strategies for teaching. In C. Seefeldt (Ed.), *Early childhood curriculum: A review of current research*. New York: Teachers College Press, Columbia University.

Lightfoot, S. (1978). *Worlds apart: Relationships between families and schools*. New York: Basic.

Lickona, T. (1983). *Raising good children*. New York: Bantam.

Lozoff, B., Brillenham, G., Trause, M. A., Kennell, J. H., & Klaus, M. H. (1977, July). The mother-newborn relationship: Limits of adaptability. *Journal of Pediatrics, 91*.

Lytton, H. (1979). Disciplinary encounters between young boys and their mothers and fathers: Is there a contingency system? *Developmental Psychology, 15*, 256–268.

McAfee, O. (1986). Research report. Circle time: Getting past "Two Little Pumpkins." *Young Children, 40*(6), 24–29.

McCracken, J. B. (Ed.). (1986). *Reducing stress in young children's lives*. Washington, DC: NAEYC.

McDonald, D. T. (1979). *Music in our lives: The early years.* Washington, DC: NAEYC.

Meisels, S. (1985). *Developmental screening in early childhood.* Washington, DC: NAEYC.

Miller, C. S. (1984). Building self-control: Discipline for young children. *Young Children, 40*(1), 15–19.

Montessori, M. (1964). *The Montessori method.* Cambridge, MA: Robert Bentley.

Moore, S. (1982). Prosocial behavior in the early years: Parent and peer influences. In B. Spodek (Ed.), *Handbook of research in early childhood education.* New York: Free Press.

Mussen, P., & Eisenberg-Bert, N. (1977). *Roots of caring, sharing, and helping: The development of prosocial behavior in children.* San Francisco: Freeman.

NAEYC. (1982). *Early childhood teacher education guidelines for four- and five-year programs.* Washington, DC: NAEYC.

NAEYC. (1984). *Accreditation criteria and procedures of the National Academy of Early Childhood Programs.* Washington, DC: NAEYC.

NAEYC. (1985). *Guidelines for early childhood education programs in associate degree granting institutions.* Washington, DC: NAEYC.

National Institute of Education. (1984). *Becoming a nation of readers: The report of the Commission on Reading.* Washington, DC: U.S. Department of Education.

Piaget, J. (1950). *The psychology of intelligence.* London: Routledge & Kegan Paul.

Piaget, J. (1952). *The origins of intelligence in children.* (M. Cook, Trans.). New York: Norton. (Original work published 1936)

Piaget, J. (1972). *Science of education and the psychology of the child* (rev. ed.). New York: Viking. (Original work published 1965)

Powell, D. (1986). Effects of program approaches and teaching practices. *Young Children, 41*(6), 60–67.

Ramsey, P. G. (1979). Beyond "Ten Little Indians" and turkeys: Alternative approaches to Thanksgiving. *Young Children, 34*(6), 28–32, 49–52.

Ramsey, P. G. (1982). Multicultural education in early childhood. *Young Children, 37*(2), 13–24.

Read, K. H., Gardner, P., & Mahler, B. (1986). *Early childhood programs: A laboratory for human relationships* (8th ed.). New York: Holt, Rinehart & Winston.

Riley, S. S. (1984). *How to generate values in young children: Integrity, honesty, individuality, self-confidence.* Washington, DC: NAEYC.

Rogers, D. L., & Ross, D. D. (1986). Encouraging positive social interaction among young children. *Young Children, 41*(3), 12–17.

Rubin, K., & Everett, B. (1982). Social per-spective-taking in young children. In S. G. Moore & C. R. Cooper (Eds.), *The young child: Reviews of research* (Vol. 3, pp. 97–114). Washington, DC: NAEYC.

Ruopp, R., Travers, J., Glantz, F., & Coelen, C. (1979). *Children at the center. Final report of the National Day Care Study* (Vol. 1). Cambridge, MA: Abt Associates.

Sackoff, E., & Hart, R. (1984, Summer). Toys: Research and applications. *Children's Environments Quarterly,* 1–2.

Saracho, O., & Spodek, B. (Eds.). (1983). *Understanding the multicultural experience in early childhood education.* Washington, DC: NAEYC.

Schachter, F. F., & Strage, A. A. (1982). Adults' talk and children's language development. In S. G. Moore & C. R. Cooper (Eds.), *The young child: Reviews of research* (Vol. 3, pp. 79–96). Washington, DC: NAEYC.

Schaffer, H. R. (1984). *The child's entry into a social world.* Orlando, FL: Academic.

Schickedanz, J. (1986). *More than the ABCs: The early stages of reading and writing.* Washington, DC: NAEYC.

Schickedanz, J., Schickedanz, D. I., & Forsyth, P. D. (1982). *Toward understanding children.* Boston: Little, Brown.

Seefeldt, C. (1986). The visual arts. In C. Seefeldt (Ed.), *The early childhood curriculum: A review of current research.* New York: Teachers College Press, Columbia University.

Shure, M. B., & Spivack, G. (1978). *Problem-solving techniques in childrearing.* San Francisco: Jossey-Bass.

Skeen, P., Garner, A. P., & Cartwright, S. (1984). *Woodworking for young children.* Washington, DC: NAEYC.

Smith, C. A., & Davis, D. E. (1976). Teaching children non-sense. *Young Children, 34*(3), 4–11.

Smith, F. (1982). *Understanding reading.* New York: Holt, Rinehart & Winston.

Smith, F. (1985). *Reading without nonsense* (2nd ed.). New York: Teachers College Press, Columbia University.

Smith, N. (1983). *Experience and art: Teaching children to paint.* New York: Teachers College Press, Columbia University.

Souweine, J., Crimmins, S., & Mazel, C. (1981). *Mainstreaming: Ideas for teaching young children.* Washington, DC: NAEYC.

Sparling, J. (1984). *Learning games for the first three years.* New York: Walker.

Spodek, B. (1985). *Teaching in the early years* (3rd ed.). Englewood Cliffs, NJ: Prentice-Hall.

Spodek, B. (Ed.). (1986). *Today's kindergarten: Exploring its knowledge base, extending its curriculum.* New York: Teachers College Press, Columbia University.

Sponseller, D. (1982). Play and early education. In B. Spodek (Ed.), *Handbook of re-search in early childhood education.* New York: Free Press.

Sprung, B. (1978). *Perspectives on non-sexist early childhood education.* New York: Teachers College Press, Columbia University.

Sroufe, L. A. (1979). The coherence of individual development. *American Psychologist, 34,* 834–841.

Standards for educational and psychological testing. (1985). Washington, DC: American Psychological Association, American Educational Research Association, and National Council on Measurement in Education.

Stewart, I. S. (1982). The real world of teaching two-year-old children. *Young Children, 37*(5), 3–13.

Stone, J. G. (1978). *A guide to discipline* (rev. ed.). Washington, DC: NAEYC.

Uphoff, J. K., & Gilmore, J. (1985, September). *Educational Leadership, 43,* 86–90.

Veach, D. M. (1977). Choice with responsibility. *Young Children, 32*(4), 22–25.

Wallinga, C. R., & Sweaney, A. L. (1985). A sense of *real* accomplishment: Young children as productive family members. *Young Children, 41*(1), 3–9.

Warren, R. M. (1977). *Caring: Supporting children's growth.* Washington, DC: NAEYC.

Weber, E. (1984). *Ideas influencing early childhood education: A theoretical analysis.* New York: Teachers College Press, Columbia University.

Weissbourd, B. (1981). Supporting parents as people. In B. Weissbourd & J. Musick (Eds.), *Infants: Their social environments.* Washington, DC: NAEYC.

Wellman, H. M. (1982). The foundations of knowledge: Concept development in the young child. In S. G. Moore & C. R. Cooper (Eds.), *The young child: Reviews of research* (Vol. 3, pp. 115–134). Washington, DC: NAEYC.

Willert, M., & Kamii, C. (1985). Reading in kindergarten: Direct versus indirect teaching. *Young Children, 40*(4), 3–9.

Willis, A., & Ricciuti, H. (1975). *A good beginning for babies: Guidelines for group care.* Washington, DC: NAEYC.

Wolfgang, C. H., & Glickman, C. D. (1980). *Solving discipline problems.* Boston: Allyn & Bacon.

Yarrow, M. R., Scott, P. M., & Waxler, C. Z. (1973). Learning concern for others. *Developmental Psychology, 8,* 240–260.

Yarrow, M. R., & Waxler, C. Z. (1976). Dimensions and correlates of prosocial behavior in young children. *Child Development, 47,* 118–125.

Zavitkovsky, D., Baker, K. R., Berlfein, J. R., & Almy, M. (1986). *Listen to the children.* Washington, DC: NAEYC.

Ziegler, P. (1985). Saying good-bye to preschool. *Young Children, 40*(3), 11–15.

16

PART 2

Developmentally Appropriate Care for Children From Birth to Age 3

During the development of NAEYC's Criteria for center accreditation through the National Academy of Early Childhood Programs, a committee from the National Center for Clinical Infant Programs (NCCIP) reviewed the document with particular attention to the way in which the Criteria addressed the care of infants and toddlers in groups. In many cases, the accreditation Criteria are written generally, with references to developmentally appropriate activities, materials, or interactions among staff and children.

This document, written by that NCCIP committee, provides more specific details about what is appropriate for infants and toddlers in group care.

Prepared by the members of the Day Care Committee of the National Center for Clinical Infant Programs
> **J. Ronald Lally**
> **Sally Provence, M.D.**
> **Eleanor Szanton**
> **Bernice Weissbourd**

Introduction

Developmentally appropriate programs for children from birth to age 3 are distinctly different from all other types of programs—they are *not* a scaled-down version of a good program for preschool children. These program differences are determined by the unique characteristics and needs of children during the first 3 years:

- changes take place far more rapidly in infancy than during any other period in life
- during infancy, as at every other age, all areas of development—cognitive, social, emotional, and physical—are intertwined
- infants are totally dependent on adults to meet their needs
- very young children are especially vulnerable to adversity because they are less able to cope actively with discomfort or stress

We will first look at how infants develop, and then consider some of the basic elements of appropriate infant care derived from this information.

How infants and toddlers develop

The early months

All infants are unique individuals whose needs and states vary from moment to moment. Adults must sensitively respond to infants' changing signals. Consistent caregiving is vital. Schedules are adjusted according to the child's eating and sleeping rhythms. Holding and touching are determined by infants' preferences for body contact, although they depend on being carried as an introduction to sensory and motor experiences. Through these responsive interactions, infants develop a sense of a benevolent, orderly world worthy of their attention.

Newborns enter the world ready for social contact. During the first 9 months they come to distinguish friends from strangers. They initiate social interactions. They make sounds and movements that communicate pleasure, surprise, anger, disappointment, anxiety, and other feelings. They develop expectations about people's behavior based on how parents and others treat them. They thrive on frequent, responsive eye contact. They delight in hearing language and other sounds. Babies may beam or calm themselves when they are held close by adults who enjoy warm physical contact.

Through these social interactions with benevolent, affectionate adults, infants begin to develop their first positive love relationships. This development of trust and emotional security comes about because babies

Through responsive interactions, infants develop a sense of a benevolent, orderly world worthy of their attention.

learn to expect positive experiences.

Therefore, if babies are to trust us, we must quickly answer their cries of distress. We must respect their individual tempo and sensitivity—if a noise startles a baby when she or he pushes a button on the activity board, we offer another less frightening activity.

This responsive communication with adults who are attuned to children helps to encourage and expand their verbal and nonverbal responses. Children begin to learn about sensory experiences, motor actions, and expressions of feelings even when they don't understand most of the words.

For very young infants, movement itself is particularly enriching. As they move their arms, legs, and other body parts, through touching and being touched, babies begin to become more aware of their body's boundaries. They soon discover they can change what they see, hear, or feel through their own activity—how delightful to shake their foot and hear the bell on the sock jingle!

Before children can creep or crawl, they depend on adults to carry them to an interesting event (such as placing them in front of a mirror) or to bring an object or activity to them. If infants are deprived of many opportunities to sample a variety of sensory and motor experiences, their emotional and cognitive development will be hampered.

A sense of well-being and emotional security conveyed by warm and responsive adults creates a learning base from which children can benefit by even more experiences. Safe in the arms of one who cares for them, they can confidently turn the handle on a jack-in-the-box, roll a ball with sparkling shapes inside it, or investigate other intriguing objects. This sense of wonder and excitement about the world can permeate a child's approach to learning far into the future.

Crawlers and walkers

Freedom to move about safely is vital for infants who are beginning to crawl or walk. While they continue to need warmth and individual attention, infants move at their own pace away from, and back to, the security of a loving adult.

Joan, 13¾ months, and Curtis, 17 months, were playing on the floor near the bookcase. They were climbing in and out of the doll bed, scrambling over each other to do so. Then Curtis got too close to Joan, wedging her in. She cried until Gina picked her up and gave her a hug. Her good humor restored, Joan climbed on the yellow truck and half sat, half leaned on it. She inspected it as she ate a cracker, then meandered about the room and climbed into the large rocking chair, where she sat rocking again.

She approached Jerry once, and as Jerry talked to her she patted Jerry's notebook, then toddled off to crawl under the crib where she sat peering out between the bars of the lowered cribside for a minute or two. Next, she crawled out without bumping her head, stood, and toddled around the room again, looking closely at what Leslie, Curtis, and Jackie were doing, but not involving herself in any of it.

*****

Once, when Martha picked up Jackie, Joan crawled across the floor, pulled to a stand at her knee, and seemed to be letting Martha know that she didn't want her to hold Jackie. Martha reached down, patted her head, and said, "What's the matter, Joan, don't you have anything to do?" Joan seemed to be satisfied with this attention and again became involved in her investigation of available toys. She frequently returned to Martha for brief contacts, receiving a smile, a pat, or a word, after which she would resume her activity in the room.

Interpretation: Gina and Martha allowed Joan plenty of time to explore what *she* wanted to—the truck, the rocking chair, the notebook, the world from behind crib bars, and three other children. Only twice did the adults directly interact with her, but they were strategic moments: Once when she was physically uncomfortable and once when she approached. Gina responded not only by removing Joan from the source of discomfort, but also by physically reminding her she was loved. Martha, too, turned some of Joan's approaches into brief verbal exchanges, which apparently satisfied her when she seemed to need more frequent refueling.

* * *

Children's awareness of their emotions and abilities expands when a responsive adult identifies and elaborates on their feelings and perceptions, even before they talk. An adult might say, for example, "You're wondering what will happen if you try to fit that cup in the box. Will it be too big? Too little? Or j-u-s-t right?" As infants become more mobile and verbal, their secure base can be reached as much through eyes and ears as by physical contact.

In a benevolent and safe environment, mobile infants thrive when they are expected to be competent and exhibit appropriate social behaviors.

Competencies. Infants can become deeply engrossed in perfecting their many skills. In high-quality programs for infants at this stage, the children are offered choices from a wide variety of materials to play with and to explore. When children direct their own play, they see themselves as competent people—a major building block in feeling good about themselves.

Daily routines such as baths and diapering can also continue to be creative times to enhance physical growth, cognitive skills, and communication.

When provided with a wealth of experiences to choose from during the day, infants seek desired activities or objects and learn to avoid painful or fearful situations. They also begin to understand, in a practical sensorimotor way, such concepts as cause and effect; the use of tools; and familiarity with distance, spatial relationships, and perspectives. They begin to group and compare. They imitate. They develop patterns of relating to others, including adults. They express themselves vocally with increasing specificity. Therefore, they need to be encouraged to explore and learn from a rich array of activities, objects, and people.

Terry (10 months) was playing with an aluminum margarine cup and an ice cream stick. He hit the cup with the stick several times and caused it to flip over. He then used the stick to scoot the upside-down cup along the floor. For 10 minutes, he continued with great concentration, as he alternately flipped and pushed the cup and observed what happened.

Later, while in the kitchen with Kathy, who was preparing food, he discovered the dishwasher and found he could roll the lower rack in and out. He kept pushing it in and pulling it out, smiling with pleasure as he listened to the changing clatter of the dishes. He then poked about in the soap well for several minutes. All of this was done in an engrossed, exploratory manner. Kathy spoke to him occasionally and commented on what he was doing, but allowed him to carry through his project in his own way.

The development of trust and emotional security comes about because babies learn to expect positive experiences. Therefore, if babies are to trust us, we must quickly answer their cries of distress.

19

Interpretation: In this situation, Terry *was* playing with a rich array of physical stimuli, none of which were expensive toys. An empty margarine cup, an ice cream stick, and a piece of kitchen equipment were all he needed. Kathy wisely allowed him the chance to roll the rack, ready to intervene only if that activity threatened the dishes. By commenting on his activities, she enabled him to absorb what language he could—long before he was able to use language himself—to begin to put together an experience and the words that describe it.

* * *

Still later during this period, mobile infants begin to use and manipulate tools (such as dipping water with a cup), to see objects as three-dimensional (for example, climbing inside a box), and to prolong or change sounds or action (such as pulling a train back and forth with the bell clanging).

These new-found skills arise as children creep, crawl, cruise, walk, climb, and descend stairs safely. Infants develop small muscle skills when they grasp, drop, pull, push, throw, nest, finger, and mouth objects. They develop their first words, usually the names of important adults or objects, and action words. Because there are so many things to stimulate infants, sensitive adults will ensure that a good balance is maintained in the levels of intensity of play, from active . . . to quiet . . . to sleep.

Social behaviors. Mobile infants are naturally very curious about other children. Friendships begin to emerge. Because infants are not yet experienced in interacting with each other, however, they often require assistance in doing so.

Leslie had become rather adept at getting what she wanted and avoiding what she didn't. Sitting on the floor with Terry one day, she watched him playing with an hourglass full of colorful beads. She looked intently, then reached over and took it from him. Terry, who did not protest, was handed an identical toy by Jerry. Leslie again observed Terry, dropped her own hourglass, and again took his. She did this with four identical toys, always wanting the one Terry had. Finally, he protested and squealed but was unable to retain the toy against her pull. When Terry cried, Jerry, with a comment, stepped in and returned Terry's property. He separated them a little and saw that each child had a toy.

*****

Leslie and Terry, age 5 months, were sitting in the playpen with several toys. They were intently engaged with the toys while the adults were busy with other children. Leslie seemed oblivious of Terry's presence as she vigorously and repeatedly banged a rubber giraffe on the floor, apparently fascinated by the squeak her activity produced. When her attention was diverted by Terry's moving foot, she stared at it intently, grasped it, and

tried unsuccessfully to bring it to her mouth. With a quizzical expression, she repeatedly stared at, grasped, and released it. She was distracted briefly by the sound of the music box, then went back to Terry's foot. She seemed to become frustrated at not being able to pick it up and put it into her mouth, and started to make complaining sounds, which soon became angry crying. She was picked up and comforted by Martha, who asked her what the trouble was, and explained in a comforting voice that it was Terry's foot, not a toy, she was reaching for.

Interpretation: It is often very hard for an adult to know exactly when to intervene between children. In the first case, the caregiver monitored but *did not* intervene until Terry protested, and he neither punished nor reprimanded Leslie. Although Leslie took Terry's toys, she was probably not competing with him, nor did she necessarily want all of the toys for herself. It seems more likely that the toy Terry had was animated by his movement of it and thus more attractive than

A sense of well-being and emotional security conveyed by warm and responsive adults creates a learning base from which children can benefit by even more experiences.

In a benevolent and safe environment, mobile infants thrive when they are expected to be competent and exhibit appropriate social behaviors.

her own toy. It was as though at this stage, she was not aware of the sameness of the toys and did not realize that she could create the same movement with her own. Terry's failure to protest for a time permitted her to continue. While one does not imagine that at this age she learned anything definite about the rights of others, in this exchange she did have to adapt to the adult's intervention.

In the second case, the caregiver intervened only when Leslie became frustrated. She then responded by not only physically breaking up the frustrating situation, but also by stating why Leslie was frustrated. Even though this explanation was undoubtedly beyond Leslie's capacity to understand, she could respond to the comforting and the tone of voice which ideally contained at one and the same time, sympathy and a "this is how the world works" character.

* * *

Children's relationships can at one minute seem very sophisticated as they imitate a gentle, patient, or generous adult. At other times, fatigue, anxiety, or other distress overwhelms such young children. Adults must expect this great variability in social interaction and be prepared to guide children toward their own solutions.

One typical problem that arises when infants become mobile is the intense possessiveness that emerges when one child wants another's toy (or snack, or time with a special person). Forcing children to share, contrary to folk wisdom, is not an effective way to help children learn to share. An ample number of

toys must be provided. More importantly, children are more likely to share when generous adults share with them.

Children also must experience many attempts to negotiate ownership, so they can develop a sense of another child's perspective as well. They need to gain confidence that a shared item will be returned to them, because they are still learning that objects exist even when they are not in sight. Only in this type of accepting atmosphere will infants begin to understand the value of and reciprocity involved in the social skill called *sharing.* In a good program, adults respect children's choice to share only when the children are willing to do so.

Toddlers and 2-year-olds

Competencies. Toddlers and 2-year-olds thrive on exploration and creativity. They enjoy fantasy (such as pretending a toy dog is alive or using a piece of cloth as a blanket), when props are selected to encourage productive play. When their needs have been met appropriately as infants, toddlers are experienced in making choices and implementing their own ideas.

Toddlers' imagination and curiosity give them great energy and creative potential. They need opportunities to develop and express these capacities. Toddlers rely on adults to help them deal with their intense feelings and rapid fluctuations in moods. Adults must be especially careful to give toddlers many chances to figure things out for themselves, while remaining available to them if they ask for assistance.

Toddlers begin to divide objects into categories. For example, they might line up all the large rubber animals for a parade and leave the small ones in the zoo. Unstructured materials for art, music, dance, and dramatic play enable children to enjoy the process of creating their own ideas and solving their own problems.

Toddlers are entering a new phase of mental activity. In addition to growing familiarity with symbols, they speak with increasing sophistication. Out of these early, relatively abstract ideas will come an understanding of adult words, numbers, and linguistic and scientific symbols. Toddlers need experiences in the use of common language and shared meaning.

The thinking of toddlers is very different from that of older children or adults. For example, they believe that all moving things are alive. The period from 18 to 36 months is filled with exploration, questioning, discovery, and a continual determination to find meaning in events, objects, and ideas.

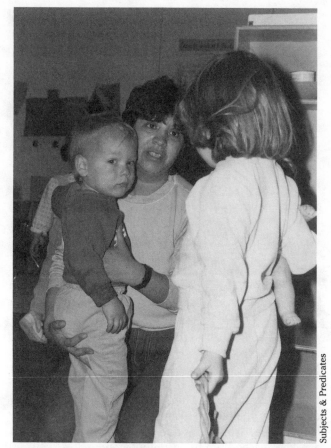

Children's relationships can at one minute seem very sophisticated as they imitate a gentle, patient, or generous adult. At other times, fatigue, anxiety, or other distress overwhelms such young children.

Gina brought a small scooter into the room and Jackie (11 months) took it immediately. He pushed it as he crawled behind it, turned it over, examined it carefully, and pulled to a stand on it and pushed it as he walked behind. Even when it tipped over, causing him to fall, he was undaunted and continued his pursuit. For 10 or 15 minutes he pushed, pulled, tipped over, and uprighted the scooter before discovering how to climb on it. Then, seated on it, he soon discovered how to push it backward. He was delighted with his newfound toy and Gina responded to his pleasure with animation and encouraging comments. He smiled and gurgled, making almost continuous "ooh" sounds in a soft, happy voice.

Interpretation: The importance of the presence of an intelligent, benevolent, and affectionate adult in facilitating infants' development cannot be overemphasized. Developmental progress occurs through a process of interaction between children and their environment, especially with the adults who care for them. Experiences in which they acquire a new skill or master some developmental task are a part of development. The adult should be able to judge children's abilities and decide how to help and support them.

Gina encouraged, supported, and appreciated Jackie's many activities with the scooter. Jackie must have experienced pleasure in learning while observing the different things that happened to the scooter in relation to his manipulation of it. Freedom to use his initiative and curiosity was important; interference from another might have robbed him of the experience of examination, evaluation, trial, and mastery in this situation. Gina protected him from intrusion and encour-

aged him. There was no doubt about his pleasure in what he was doing or that he had learned something. An astronomer discovering a planet could not have been more eloquent in communicating the excitement and joy of discovery.

* * *

Once we understand that toddlers learn by active involvement with people and by manipulating objects, it becomes clear that such activities as coloring books, worksheets, and models made of clay or other materials that children are expected to imitate are inappropriate.

Toilet learning frequently becomes the paramount issue during the third year of life. Parents and staff should agree upon an approach for helping children learn this new aspect of self-control. Professionals must ensure that common, but inappropriate, techniques such as punishment or shaming children, are not used in the child care setting. Toilet learning can only be effective if the child wants to learn, and feels responsible. It must be accomplished in a spirit of co-operation and enthusiasm as children reach this milestone in their development.

With David, the course of toilet learning was not entirely smooth, though not really difficult. The staff began suggesting that he might like to go to the potty when he was 19 months and started removing his diaper and putting him on the potty chair. The first day he usually wet himself as his diaper was being removed. However, on the second day he had a bowel movement on the pot and seemed very pleased with himself. For the next few days he would occasionally urinate or defecate in the pot with some pleasure.

Then he entered a period when he wasn't sure the whole thing was a good idea at all. At 20½ months, when asked to go to the pot, he answered vehemently, "No pot, no pot!" He was taken anyway but did nothing, though a few minutes after he was off the potty and back in his training pants, he wet himself.

Then for a time David's attendance was irregular, making it more difficult for him and the staff to pursue his toilet learning in the center. At 26 months, he adamantly refused the pot and efforts were simply suspended for a time. A note was made that he did not mind being wet and did not indicate any wish to be changed when wet. However, he was not protesting the change of diapers and was very lively and happy, interacting in a playful way with Kathy, his major caregiver.

When he was 26½ months, an observation which suggested that his oppositional behavior had something specific to do with Kathy as well as with his mother was made. While he would not go to the potty for Kathy, he would allow any one of three other staff members to take him and seemed very happy and pleased with himself at such times. This is a good example of a typical kind of struggle often seen around toilet learning: The child wishes both to learn and not to learn to use the toilet, and may express one side of his feelings with one person and the other side with others. Responding to this cue from David, we arranged that for a time he be taken to the potty by someone other than Kathy. He then began to ask to be taken and to be pleased with his own mastery. At 27 months, he was using the toilet willingly, standing to urinate, and was wearing a diaper only at naptime. A week later, the note was made that the only time he wet himself was while napping, but he rejected any attempt to put a diaper on during his nap. By the time another week had passed, he either took himself to the bathroom or asked to be taken, having gained full control and having assumed responsibility for self-regulation in this area.

*****

Larry, 25 months, was sitting in the wooden carriage next to the sandbox. He began to look very sad and started crying. When Martha asked what was wrong, he didn't answer. When she picked him up she discovered he was wet. He had been asked several times during the morning whether he wanted to go to the potty and had

Once we understand that toddlers learn by active involvement with people and by manipulating objects, it becomes clear that such activities as coloring books, worksheets, and models made of clay or other materials that children are expected to imitate, are inappropriate.

Young children come to value themselves if they have been valued.

refused each time. She took him to be changed and he cried the entire time, until she reminded him that she was not going to spank him. With that reassurance, he stopped crying while she finished dressing him, and went back to play until lunchtime.

Interpretation: In both of these situations, the caregivers followed the cues of the child and the family, continually encouraging toilet learning through reminders, actual trips to the potty, and praise, but without punishment or shaming when expectations were not met.

* * *

Social behaviors. The social awareness of toddlers and 2-year-olds is vastly more complex than that of younger infants. Their past experiences in communicating with others enable them to refine their ability to read children's and adults' signals. Their feelings of empathy bloom as they continue to see that other people have feelings too. They increasingly imitate others.

One of the most important sources of toddlers' self-esteem is the continuity of relationships with loving adults. Young children come to value themselves if they have been valued. This esteem in turn makes them receptive to positive guidance. If adults have realistic expectations, and communicate them clearly and consistently, toddlers and 2-year-olds learn and accept the limits of appropriate and inappropriate behavior.

While they rely on adult protection and guidance, toddlers assert their awareness of their separateness from others. They feel independent and competent, and yet they realize they will depend on adults. A healthy toddler's inner world is filled with conflicting feelings—independence and dependence, pride and shame, confidence and doubt, self-awareness and confusion, fear and omnipotence, hostility and intense love, anger and tenderness, initiative and passivity. These feelings challenge parents' and staff resourcefulness and knowledge to provide emotional security.

For this age group, sound emotional development is derived from experiences that support initiative, creativity, autonomy, and self-esteem and yet recognize that the children are still very young. Toddlers strive to be independent and self-reliant, and yet they need to count on affection and comfort.

Toddlers and 2-year-olds need opportunities to be responsible, to make significant choices, and to be challenged or disciplined in ways that keep their dignity intact. They are beginning to understand why certain behavior must be limited—that rules are fair and judgments just. They need to feel these limits are placed on them by adults who can be counted on and who mean what they say. These are adults who can support them in their frustrations and disappointments and enjoy their pleasures and successes with them.

They need guidance in how to express their often intense and hostile feelings in acceptable ways. If toddlers and 2-year-olds do not have the guidance of adults who understand and plan appropriately for them, they may experience severe stress and conflict. A group of young children without adequate adult support can become a chaotic environment in which child development is severely impaired. The next section will examine the details of the basic elements in appropriate infant care.

Basic elements of appropriate care for infants and toddlers

Particularly in the preverbal and early verbal years, observations of child behavior, and of child-adult and child-child interaction, provide essential information about children and their caregivers. Assessments about the extent to which the adult, whether parent or other caregiver, is in tune with a child and whether a child is progressing in a healthy manner are derived in large measure from observation augmented by insights and information provided by the adults who know the child best—usually parents.

General knowledge about infants and young children from theoretical, philosophical, and practical sources provides a necessary conceptual framework. Within that framework, however, one must have the benefit of seeing and knowing the individual child in order to plan, provide, and evaluate those experiences that will facilitate healthy development.

For the first few months of life, warm, supportive, and dependable adult-child contact is essential if infants are to develop a sense of security and trust. As infants begin to crawl, they use these early feelings of confidence and competence to explore new environments. They also must have the opportunity to return safely to the base of a readily available, loving caregiver.

Then as older toddlers and 2-year-olds, children who are secure and trusting will be increasingly ready to take initiative, be creative, participate in a group, and assert themselves as individuals. An atmosphere of affectionate attention is essential for healthy development throughout childhood.

What kinds of interactions and activities are characteristic of this type of atmosphere?

Patient, warm adults

Patient, warm adults are probably the most important factor in a developmentally appropriate program for infants and toddlers. From birth, children take an active role in their interaction with others. Adults who work well with children younger than age 3 are aware of the need to mesh their behaviors with each child's unique style of approaching people and objects.

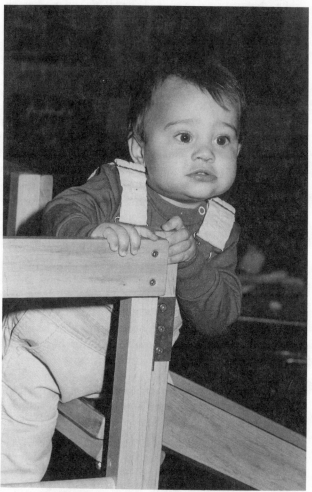

Toddlers and 2-year-olds need opportunities to be responsible, to make significant choices, and to be challenged or disciplined in ways that keep their dignity intact.

25

Routines are the curriculum. The following examples illustrate how important it is to make the most of every minute of a young child's day.

> When put in his highchair for lunch, Jackie (10 months) was quiet. He remained so while Joan (13 months), who was hungry and irritable, was put in her chair. As soon as he saw her plate of food, however, Jackie began to fuss and kick impatiently. Gina put some bits of corned beef hash and green beans on his tray, and he quieted for about 5 minutes as he picked up small pieces with his thumb and index finger, and ate them.
>
> Once in a while, he stopped eating to look at Joan. He listened as Gina talked with Joan about what she was eating and about how well Joan was using her spoon. As Gina began to feed Jackie, he reached toward her mouth with a bean, then smiled with pleasure when she ate it and said, "Oh, that's good Jackie. Thank you." A bit later, while he was fed pudding, he insisted on holding the spoon so Gina took another.
>
> Joan, by now, was beginning to smear her food on her highchair tray. Gina did not interfere. With help from Gina, Jackie held a small glass of milk and took a sip or two, but managed to spill much of it. He slid down in his chair, rubbed his eyes, appeared sleepy, and pulled at his bib. Gina took him out of the chair and held him on her lap as she helped Joan finish her meal. Joan then played on the floor as Gina washed Jackie's hands and face and got him ready for his nap.

Interpretation: Gina knew from her observations that Jackie was able to pick up small bits of food and feed himself, and she set things up to allow him to do so. Joan, just 3 months older, had more capacity for self-feeding than Jackie. Gina's ability to keep contact with both children was noteworthy. She was there to give help to each child as needed, to encourage self-feeding, and to keep the meal pleasant. It is very hard for most young children, even after they are capable of self-feeding, to do so without adult support.

The art of being available to help children eat while also allowing them to work at self-feeding is not easy for some adults. There is a tendency to either do it all for the child or to expect the child to do it alone. Time, patience, and the capacity to be pleased with gradual change are required. The adult must also be able to accept some messiness as the child handles and smears the food.

* * *

Even newborns sense whether someone enjoys their company during play and everyday routines such as diapering.

> Martha was bathing Leslie (4 months), who was happy, smiling, and relaxed as Martha talked with her. Leslie reached for a container of shampoo nearby. Martha moved it out of reach and put a small, red plastic fish into the water to attract Leslie's attention. She looked at it intently, moved her arms, and tried to reach and grasp it, splashing the water. This activity seemed to fascinate

her and she continued to splash more and more actively, squealing with delight. A little later, she watched intently as Martha squeezed water out of the sponge. Before her bath was finished she succeeded, after several attempts, in grasping the floating fish with both hands.

*****

> Jackie (8½ months) was sitting quietly in a large, deep sink playing with a plastic shampoo bottle while Gina washed his hair. He soon reached for the soap dish and the plastic cup on the counter until he managed to get both of them into the water. He enjoyed manipulating them as they floated about. Twice he pulled to a stand by holding the edge of the sink, smiling broadly. At one point, smiling, he held the cup out toward the observer as to show it to her. When Joan (11 months) approached the sink and put her hand on the counter, Jackie touched her hand, smiled, and gurgled at her.
>
> Gina lifted Jackie from the water and placed him on the counter to be dried. He seemed to enjoy being rubbed with the towel. He smiled at Gina, and made happy squeals and a "da da" sound. He remained inactive, lying on his back while his diaper and shirt were put on. Gina talked with him frequently while she bathed and dressed him and Jackie responded by making soft, pleasant sounds. When placed in a sitting position to have the rest of his clothes put on, he did not try to move away, nor did he actively enter the dressing process. When he was dressed, Gina helped him stand up and invited him to look at himself in the mirror. He smiled, babbled, and waved his hand at the observer, whose reflection he could also see. He then looked at his own reflection, smiled broadly, and bounced up and down as though charmed with what he saw.

Interpretation: With infants and toddlers, giving baths, changing diapers, and dressing are frequent experiences during the day. Being bathed or dressed is as much a part of the curriculum for the infant as working a puzzle, looking at a book, building a house, or counting is for an older child. When viewed from this perspective, adults can think about how these experiences can promote an infant's development.

Infants care little about being clean or sweet-smelling, but they do relish and learn from the social contact and from varied sensations as they experience changes in temperature, texture, position, sight, sound, and smell. Because baths call for close adult attention, they are a marvelous opportunity to talk to infants about themselves, what is going on, what the infants are doing, and how they are feeling. A person who enjoys infants can easily see how the bath experience can be used to stimulate learning in a perfectly natural and informal manner.

The caregivers in each of these situations use the bathing and drying process as a time to allow the child to experiment with the behavior of objects in the water and with the properties of water. Leslie practiced how to successfully grasp a floating object—a great accom-

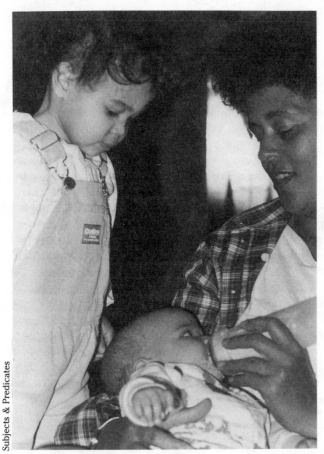

Patient, warm adults are probably the most important factor in a developmentally appropriate program for infants and toddlers.

plishment. Jackie practiced how to move his body in water. Gina used the drying process to express warmth, both physically and verbally. When Jackie saw his own body in the mirror, he was putting together what he felt with what he saw. In both cases, the infant engaged in sensorimotor learning and mastery play in association with enjoying positive social interaction with the adult.

Relating to others. Infants pick up on body language long before they can communicate verbally. Age-appropriate behaviors such as crying, messiness, dependency, willfulness, aggression, and curiosity about genital differences may make some adults uncomfortable. However, when we know these characteristics are typical, we can support infant development rather than deal with these behaviors through anger or punishment.

Curtis, 15 months, was in the playroom with Shaun, Jackie, and Joan. He silently pushed the block cart first into Jackie and then into Joan. Although an adult tried to direct him to push in another direction, he persisted in bumping into the children. He then abandoned the cart, toddled to Jackie, and pushed him over. Jackie protested by whining. Curtis moved on to Joan and tried to push her over also, but she squealed loudly and grabbed his overalls, almost pulling him down.

A few minutes later, he was sitting on the floor when Joan approached him. He reached out, grasped the seat of her pants, and pulled her down, all the time ignoring the observant adult's admonitions not to do so because it would hurt. The children were separated and he was given a jack-in-the-box, which he explored deliberately. He then spent about 2 minutes toddling about holding a squeaky toy. When he made it squeak, he smiled and looked at Karen. She smiled and commented on his making the toy squeak.

Several other times during the next hour he approached and pushed, bumped, or took toys away from smaller children. He hit at Shaun and pulled his hair. Later, he began to cry woefully. Karen went to him and he quieted briefly, then crawled a few feet away from her, lay on the floor, and broke into loud, sorrowful wails. As she soothingly talked to him, rocked him, and patted his cheek, he stopped crying and rested his head on her arm, still sobbing occasionally. He cried while she put his coat on, but once outside he was quiet while she pushed him in a cart. He was relaxed and solemn with a sorrowful expression on his face.

Interpretation: Only at the end of the morning did the several adults who had intervened to protect the other children from Curtis fully realize how many times aggressive contact was made. This situation might occur with any child of this age on any day. The adults realized that Curtis had been having difficulty adjusting to the program, so his caregiver tried to provide him with support and comfort and to help him play.

Curtis's behavior illustrates the typical difficulties young children have coping with stress. While the caregivers did not know what was going on in Curtis's mind, he was clearly unhappy much of the day and needed comfort and reassurance from his special caregiver. A young child who is unhappy and agitated, and who feels dissatisfied with adults, may be more aggressive toward other children. While Curtis's aggressive behavior had to be controlled, he needed consolation and help, not punishment.

* * *

Only by seeing that the continuity and consistency of our affectionate care is essential for children's development can we make informed decisions about the type of program we offer. Through their experiences with adults and other children, infants start the lifelong process of learning about themselves and how to get along with others. Their first feelings of empathy and mutual respect emerge when they are a part of sensitive and timely verbal and nonverbal communication.

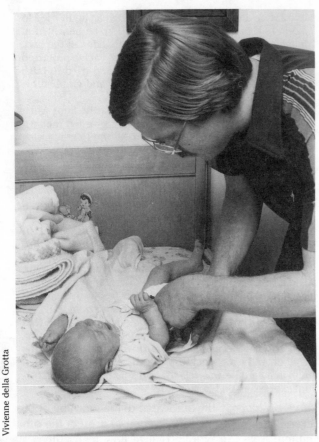

Vivienne della Grotta

Even newborns sense whether someone enjoys their company during play and everyday routines.

Because some of the most basic elements of ethnic identity are established before age 3, infants and toddlers thrive in a setting that is culturally salient. Caregivers must recognize and support what is unique, and possibly culturally inspired, about each child. Children benefit greatly when parents and caregivers frequently and respectfully consult with each other.

Very young children also need opportunities to learn from other parts of the world around them—through a variety of colors, odors, sounds, materials, and tastes. Much of the time they play alone or in the company of a few other children. Adults who understand how children learn recognize that children gain from every experience as they initiate activities, explore new situations, engage in messy activities such as water play, use art materials, and respond to music and words.

Growth simply cannot be divided into social, emotional, physical, and cognitive development during these early years. Each child's development is individual, characterized by her or his own particular leaps, plateaus, and regressions.

Responsiveness to physical needs

Very young children cannot survive if we do not provide shelter, food, and other essential comforts. *How* these elements of survival are provided strongly affects how children see themselves and their value as people. Children come to expect an orderly world and feel motivated to develop self-control if they sense that adults respond to these physical needs as quickly as possible and with affection.

Accidents are the greatest cause of death for infants who are mobile. For this reason, their curiosity must be safely channeled without being smothered and their environment tailored to ensure their safety. All the indoor and outdoor areas, the equipment, toys, and furniture in a good program are designed to ensure children's safety, while promoting their urge to explore. Activities are monitored by a nearby adult, too.

Children can gradually be helped to learn what is safe, what is dangerous, and why. Children in a rocking boat, for example, can learn to stop rocking if another child comes near, so their fingers or feet don't get hurt. Once again, children sense they are important when they feel safe and know they will be comforted if they are injured. They also come to realize that others are similarly important.

Programs that support families

Mutual support and good communication are essential between parents and program staff. During these earliest years, children learn whether their environment is supportive, ordered, and predictable. Parents and staff who share information frequently about children's routines, unique behaviors, and daily events contribute to this sense of support.

If parents or caregivers compete with or resent each other, infants will feel the tension. Most parents have some guilt and anxiety about leaving their children in the care of another person. However, by showing support for parents as the prime adults in their children's lives, these tensions can be greatly diminished. By developing a partnership, adults see the child from a shared perspective. It is especially important that parents and caregivers discuss basic values and childrearing practices. Without such communication, children may become bewildered, confused, and anxious if there are major discrepancies between what happens at home and in the caregiving environment.

When adults share details about a child, everyone has a greater sense of the child's emerging individuality. Knowing how long a child slept or how much formula was consumed or what the child enjoyed playing with, for example, is valuable information in planning the day or evening.

As infants reach the middle of their first year, it is natural for them to become anxious around strangers, such as when their parents leave them with an unfamiliar caregiver. Stranger anxiety is a sign that children are maturing emotionally, cognitively, and socially. In a good program, parents and staff anticipate this stage and find ways to ease the difficult period, perhaps by engaging the child with an interesting toy rather than by establishing direct physical contact.

In the months that follow, as children begin to crawl and then to walk, they are better able to explore and indicate their preferences. Their favorite toys, foods, and activities can be sources of pride and interest for parents and staff alike. Infants flourish when they see their new skills appreciated by people who are important to them.

At this stage of development, the limits on their activities should be reasonably consistent between home and program. These limits, whenever possible, should be reached by mutual agreement. Parents and staff will want to talk about what activities can be encouraged at home, or how favorite foods from home might be introduced in the program.

Toddlers, too, need stable environments and understanding adults in their struggle for independence while they cling to babyhood. They work to control their emotions, which shift quickly from one extreme to another. They strive to master emerging skills that

Good programs for children from birth to age 3 are distinctly different from all other types of programs—they are *not* a scaled-down version of a good program for preschool children.

are both pleasantly exciting and anxiety-producing. Toddlers often develop their own rituals and routines to help themselves feel organized and secure.

Parents and caregivers who share knowledge about toddlers respect these developmental patterns. They should frequently discuss major events such as emotional outbursts, triumphs, and creative endeavors. In doing so, both the home and the child care program can agree on ways to provide a dependable environment that supports toddlers as they define themselves. Joint planning for toilet learning is certainly one of the most important areas that parents and teachers can collaborate on later in toddlerhood.

Summary

Infants and toddlers learn through their own experience, trial and error, repetition, imitation, and identification. Adults guide and encourage this learning by ensuring that the environment is safe and emotionally supportive. An appropriate program for children younger than age 3 invites play, active exploration, and movement. It provides a broad array of stimulating experiences within a reliable framework of routines and protection from excessive stress. Relationships with people are emphasized as an essential contribution to the quality of children's experiences.

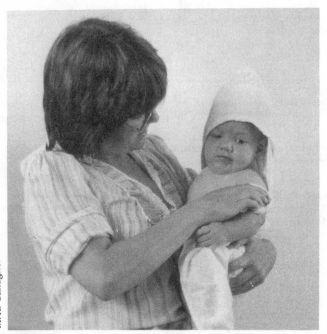

M. K. Gallagher

Being bathed or dressed is as much a part of the curriculum for the infant as working a puzzle, looking at a book, building a house, or counting is for an older child.

	Interest in others	Self-awareness	Motor milestones and eye-hand skills
The Early Months (birth through 8 months)	Newborns prefer the human face and human sound. Within the first 2 weeks, they recognize and prefer the sight, smell, and sound of the principal caregiver. Social smile and mutual gazing is evidence of early social interaction. The infant can initiate and terminate these interactions. Anticipates being lifted or fed and moves body to participate. Sees adults as objects of interest and novelty. Seeks out adults for play. Stretches arms to be taken.	Sucks fingers or hand fortuitously. Observes own hands. Places hand up as an object comes close to the face as if to protect self. Looks to the place on body where being touched. Reaches for and grasps toys. Clasps hands together and fingers them. Tries to cause things to happen. Begins to distinguish friends from strangers. Shows preference for being held by familiar people.	The young infant uses many complex reflexes: searches for something to suck; holds on when falling; turns head to avoid obstruction of breathing; avoids brightness, strong smells, and pain. Puts hand or object in mouth. Begins reaching toward interesting objects. Grasps, releases, regrasps, and releases object again. Lifts head. Holds head up. Sits up without support. Rolls over. Transfers and manipulates objects with hands. Crawls.
Crawlers and Walkers (8 to 18 months)	Exhibits anxious behavior around unfamiliar adults. Enjoys exploring objects with another as the basis for establishing relationships. Gets others to do things for child's pleasure (wind up toys, read books, get dolls). Shows considerable interest in peers. Demonstrates intense attention to adult language.	Knows own name. Smiles or plays with self in mirror. Uses large and small muscles to explore confidently when a sense of security is offered by presence of caregiver. Frequently checks for caregiver's presence. Has heightened awareness of opportunities to make things happen, yet limited awareness of responsibility for own actions. Indicates strong sense of self through assertiveness. Directs actions of others (e.g., "Sit there!"). Identifies one or more body parts. Begins to use *me, you, I.*	Sits well in chairs. Pulls self up, stands holding furniture. Walks when led. Walks alone. Throws objects. Climbs stairs. Uses marker on paper. Stoops, trots, can walk backward a few steps.
Toddlers and 2-Year-Olds (18 months to 3 years)	Shows increased awareness of being seen and evaluated by others. Sees others as a barrier to immediate gratification. Begins to realize others have rights and privileges. Gains greater enjoyment from peer play and joint exploration. Begins to see benefits of cooperation. Identifies self with children of same age or sex. Is more aware of the feelings of others. Exhibits more impulse control and self-regulation in relation to others. Enjoys small group activities.	Shows strong sense of self as an individual, as evidenced by "NO" to adult requests. Experiences self as a powerful, potent, creative doer. Explores everything. Becomes capable of self-evaluation and has beginning notions of self (good, bad, attractive, ugly). Makes attempts at self-regulation. Uses names of self and others. Identifies 6 or more body parts.	Scribbles with marker or crayon. Walks up and down stairs. Can jump off one step. Kicks a ball. Stands on one foot. Threads beads. Draws a circle. Stands and walks on tiptoes. Walks up stairs one foot on each step. Handles scissors. Imitates a horizontal crayon stroke.

Note: *This list is not intended to be exhaustive. Many of the behaviors indicated here will happen earlier or later for individual infants. The chart suggests an approximate time when a behavior might appear, but it should not be rigidly interpreted.*

Often, but not always, the behaviors appear in the order in which they emerge. Particularly for younger infants, the behaviors listed in one domain overlap considerably with several other developmental domains. Some behaviors are placed under more than one category to emphasize this interrelationship.

CHILDREN FROM BIRTH TO AGE 3

Language development/ communication	Physical, spatial, and temporal awareness	Purposeful action and use of tools	Expression of feelings
Cries to signal pain or distress. Smiles or vocalizes to initiate social contact. Responds to human voices. Gazes at faces. Uses vocal and nonvocal communication to express interest and exert influence. Babbles using all types of sounds. Engages in private conversations when alone. Combines babbles. Understands names of familiar people and objects. Laughs. Listens to conversations.	Comforts self by sucking thumb or finding pacifier. Follows a slowly moving object with eyes. Reaches and grasps toys. Looks for dropped toy. Identifies objects from various viewpoints. Finds a toy hidden under a blanket when placed there while watching.	Observes own hands. Grasps rattle when hand and rattle are both in view. Hits or kicks an object to make a pleasing sight or sound continue. Tries to resume a knee ride by bouncing to get adult started again.	Expresses discomfort and comfort/ pleasure unambiguously. Responds with more animation and pleasure to primary caregiver than to others. Can usually be comforted by familiar adult when distressed. Smiles and activates the obvious pleasure in response to social stimulation. Very interested in people. Shows displeasure at loss of social contact. Laughs aloud (belly laugh). Shows displeasure or disappointment at loss of toy. Expresses several clearly differentiated emotions: pleasure, anger, anxiety or fear, sadness, joy, excitement, disappointment, exuberance. Reacts to strangers with soberness or anxiety.
Understands many more words than can say. Looks toward 20 or more objects when named. Creates long babbled sentences. Shakes head no. Says 2 or 3 clear words. Looks at picture books with interest, points to objects. Uses vocal signals other than crying to gain assistance. Begins to use *me, you, I*.	Tries to build with blocks. If toy is hidden under 1 of 3 cloths while child watches, looks under the right cloth for the toy. Persists in a search for a desired toy even when toy is hidden under distracting objects such as pillows. When chasing a ball that rolled under sofa and out the other side, will make a detour around sofa to get ball. Pushes foot into shoe, arm into sleeve.	When a toy winds down, continues the activity manually. Uses a stick as a tool to obtain a toy. When a music box winds down, searches for the key to wind it up again. Brings a stool to use for reaching for something. Pushes away someone or something not wanted. Feeds self finger food (bits of fruit, crackers). Creeps or walks to get something or avoid unpleasantness. Pushes foot into shoe, arm into sleeve. Partially feeds self with fingers or spoon. Handles cup well with minimal spilling. Handles spoon well for self-feeding.	Actively shows affection for familiar person: hugs, smiles at, runs toward, leans against, and so forth. Shows anxiety at separation from primary caregiver. Shows anger focused on people or objects. Expresses negative feelings. Shows pride and pleasure in new accomplishments. Shows intense feelings for parents. Continues to show pleasure in mastery. Asserts self, indicating strong sense of self.
Combines words. Listens to stories for a short while. Speaking vocabulary may reach 200 words. Develops fantasy in language. Begins to play pretend games. Defines use of many household items. Uses compound sentences. Uses adjectives and adverbs. Recounts events of the day.	Identifies a familiar object by touch when placed in a bag with 2 other objects. Uses "tomorrow," "yesterday." Figures out which child is missing by looking at children who are present. Asserts independence: "Me do it." Puts on simple garments such as cap or slippers.	When playing with a ring-stacking toy, ignores any forms that have no hole. Stacks only rings or other objects with holes. Classifies, labels, and sorts objects by group (hard versus soft, large versus small). Helps dress and undress self.	Frequently displays aggressive feelings and behaviors. Exhibits contrasting states and mood shifts (stubborn versus compliant). Shows increased fearfulness (dark, monsters, etc.). Expresses emotions with increasing control. Aware of own feelings and those of others. Shows pride in creation and production. Verbalizes feelings more often. Expresses feelings in symbolic play. Shows empathic concern for others.

For more information about programs for infants and toddlers:

Bell, S., & Ainsworth, M. D. S. (1972). Infant crying and maternal responsiveness. *Child Development, 43,* 1171–1190.

Brazelton, T. B. (1976). *Toddlers and parents: A declaration of independence.* New York: Dell.

Brazelton, T. B. (1983). *Infants and mothers: Differences in development.* New York: Delacorte.

Brazelton, T. B. (1983). *Working and caring.* Reading, MA: Addison-Wesley.

Brazelton, T. B. (1984). Cementing family relationships through child care. In L. Dittmann (Ed.), *The infants we care for* (rev. ed.). Washington, DC: NAEYC.

Brown, C. C. (Ed.). (1981). *Infants at risk: Assessment and intervention.* Skillman, NJ: Johnson & Johnson Baby Products Company Pediatric Round Table Series.

Cazden, C. (Ed.). (1981). *Language in early childhood education* (rev. ed.). Washington, DC: NAEYC.

Chance, P. (Ed.). (1979). *Learning through play.* Skillman, NJ: Johnson & Johnson Baby Products Company Pediatric Round Table Series.

Dittmann, L. (1984). *The infants we care for.* Washington, DC: NAEYC.

Erikson, E. (1950). *Childhood and society.* New York: Norton.

Fein, G., & Rivkin, M. (Eds.). (1986). *The young child at play: Reviews of research* (Vol. 4). Washington, DC: NAEYC.

Genishi, C. (1986). Acquiring language and communicative competence. In C. Seefeldt (Ed.), *Early childhood curriculum: A review of current research.* New York: Teachers College Press, Columbia University.

Gerber, M. (1982). What is appropriate curriculum for infants and toddlers? In B. Weissbourd & J. Musick (Eds.), *Infants: Their social environments.* Washington, DC: NAEYC.

Gonzalez-Mena, J. (1986). Toddlers: What to expect. *Young Children, 42*(1), 47–51.

Gonzalez-Mena, J., & Eyer, D. W. (1980). *Infancy and caregiving.* Palo Alto, CA: Mayfield.

Gordon, T. (1970). *Parent effectiveness training.* New York: Wyden.

Gordon, T. (1975). *Teacher effectiveness training.* New York: McKay.

Green, M. I. (1984). *A sign of relief.* Des Plaines, IL: Bantam.

Greenfield, P. M., & Tronick, E. (1980). *Infant curriculum, the Bromley-Health guide to the care of infants in groups.* Santa Monica, CA: Good Year Publishing.

Greenspan, S., & Greenspan, N. T. (1985). *First feelings: Milestones in the emotional development of your baby and child.* New York: Viking.

Hoffman, M. L. (1975). Moral internalization, parental power, and the nature of parent-child interaction. *Developmental Psychology, 11,* 228–239.

Honig, A. S. (1981). What are the needs of infants? *Young Children, 37*(1), 3–10.

Honig, A. S. (1982). Parent involvement in early childhood education. In B. Spodek (Ed.), *Handbook of research in early childhood education.* New York: Free Press.

Honig, A. S. (1985). High quality infant/toddler care. *Young Children, 41*(1), 40–46.

Honig, A. S., & Lally, R. (1981). *Infant caregiving: A design for training.* Syracuse, NY: Syracuse University Press.

Katz, L. (1980). Mothering and teaching: Some significant distinctions. In L. Katz (Ed.), *Current topics in early childhood education* (Vol. 3, pp. 47–64). Norwood, NJ: Ablex.

Kopp, C. B. (1982). Antecedents of self-regulation: A developmental perspective. *Developmental Psychology, 18,* 199–214.

Klaus, M. H., Leger, T., & Trause, M. A. (Eds.). (1975). *Maternal attachment and mothering disorders: A round table.* Skillman, NJ: Johnson & Johnson Baby Products Company Pediatric Round Table Series.

Klaus, M., & Robertson, M. O. (Eds.). (1982). *Birth, interaction and attachment.* Skillman, NJ: Johnson & Johnson Baby Products Company Pediatric Round Table Series.

Kuczynski, L. (1983). Reasoning, prohibitions, and motivations for compliance. *Developmental Psychology, 19,* 126–134.

Lansky, V. (1974). *Feed me! I'm yours.* Deephaven, MN: Meadowbrook.

Lightfoot, S. (1978). *Worlds apart: Relationships between families and schools.* New York: Basic.

Lozoff, B., Brillenham, G., Trause, M. A., Kennell, J. H., & Klaus, M. H. (1977). The mother-newborn relationship: Limits of adaptability. *Journal of Pediatrics, 91.*

McDonald, D. T. (1979). *Music in our lives: The early years.* Washington, DC: NAEYC.

Miller, C. S. (1984). Building self-control: Discipline for

young children. *Young Children, 40*(1), 15–19.

Moore, S. (1982). Prosocial behavior in the early years: Parent and peer influences. In B. Spodek (Ed.), *Handbook of research in early childhood education.* New York: Free Press.

Mussen, P., & Eisenberg-Bert, N. (1977). *Roots of caring, sharing, and helping: The development of prosocial behavior in children.* San Francisco: Freeman.

Piaget, J. (1950). *The psychology of intelligence.* London: Routledge & Kegan Paul.

Piaget, J. (1952). *The origins of intelligence in children.* (M. Cook, Trans.). New York: Norton. (Original work published 1936)

Princeton Center for Infancy. (1974). *The first twelve months of life: Your baby's growth month by month.* New York: Grosset & Dunlap.

Reilly, A. P. (Ed.). (1980). *The communication game.* Skillman, NJ: Johnson & Johnson Baby Products Company Pediatric Round Table Series.

Riley, S. S. (1984). *How to generate values in young children: Integrity, honesty, individuality, self-confidence.* Washington, DC: NAEYC.

Rogers, D. L., & Ross, D. D. (1986). Encouraging positive social interaction among young children. *Young Children, 41*(3), 12–17.

Rubin, K., & Everett, B. (1982). Social perspective-taking in young children. In S. G. Moore & C. R. Cooper (Eds.), *The young child: Reviews of research* (Vol. 3, pp. 97–114). Washington, DC: NAEYC.

Ruopp, R., Travers, J., Glantz, F., & Coelen, C. (1979). *Children at the center. Final report of the National Day Care Study* (Vol. 1). Cambridge, MA: Abt Associates.

Sackoff, E., & Hart, R. (1984, Summer). Toys: Research and applications. *Children's Environments Quarterly,* 1–2.

Sasserath, V. J., & Hoekelman, R. A. (1983). *Child health care communications.* Skillman, NJ: Johnson & Johnson Baby Products Company Pediatric Round Table Series.

Schachter, F. F., & Strage, A. A. (1982). Adults' talk and children's language development. In S. G. Moore & C. R. Cooper (Eds.), *The young child: Reviews of research* (Vol. 3, pp. 79–96). Washington, DC: NAEYC.

Schaffer, H. R. (1984). *The child's entry into a social world.* Orlando, FL: Academic.

Schickedanz, J. (1986). *More than the ABCs: The early stages of reading and writing.* Washington, DC: NAEYC.

Schickedanz, J., Schickedanz, D. I., & Forsyth, P. D. (1982). *Toward understanding children.* Boston: Little, Brown.

Segal, M. (1974). *From birth to one year.* Fort Lauderdale: Nova University.

Segal, M., & Adcock, D. (1976). *From one to two years.* Fort Lauderdale: Nova University.

Smith, C. A., & Davis, D. E. (1976). Teaching children non-sense. *Young Children, 34*(3), 4–11.

Sparling, J. (1984). *Learning games for the first three years.* New York: Walker.

Sprung, B. (1978). *Perspectives on non-sexist early childhood education.* New York: Teachers College Press, Columbia University.

Sroufe, L. A. (1979). The coherence of individual development. *American Psychologist, 34,* 834–841.

Stewart, I. S. (1982). The real world of teaching two-year-old children. *Young Children, 37*(5), 3–13.

Stone, J. G. (1978). *A guide to discipline* (rev. ed.). Washington, DC: NAEYC.

Thoman, E. B., & Trotter, S. (Eds.). (1978). *Social responsiveness of infants.* Skillman, NJ: Johnson & Johnson Baby Products Company Pediatric Round Table Series.

Warren, R. M. (1977). *Caring: Supporting children's growth.* Washington, DC: NAEYC.

Weissbourd, B. (1981). Supporting parents as people. In B. Weissbourd & J. Musick (Eds.), *Infants: Their social environments.* Washington, DC: NAEYC.

Wellman, H. M. (1982). The foundations of knowledge: Concept development in the young child. In S. G. Moore & C. R. Cooper (Eds.), *The young child: Reviews of research* (Vol. 3, pp. 115–134). Washington, DC: NAEYC.

White, B. (1975). *The first three years of life.* Englewood Cliffs, NJ: Prentice-Hall.

Willis, A., & Ricciuti, H. (1975). *A good beginning for babies: Guidelines for group care.* Washington, DC: NAEYC.

PART 3

Integrated Components of Developmentally Appropriate Practice for Infants and Toddlers

In Part 2 of this book, the National Center for Clinical Infant Programs and NAEYC describe the vital development that takes place during the first 3 years of life and give examples of appropriate care of infants and toddlers. Building on the previous description of development and practice, Part 3 is designed for practitioners who care for infants or toddlers in group settings. Both appropriate and inappropriate practices are described here, because people often understand a concept most clearly if they are presented both positive and negative examples.

Because all areas of development are thoroughly integrated during early childhood, the title for these descriptions refers to integrated components. The components of practice

that are referred to in this section parallel the components of a group program as described in NAEYC's Accreditation Criteria and Procedures of the National Academy of Early Childhood Programs. *It is hoped that the descriptions of appropriate and inappropriate practices that follow will help directors and teachers to interpret and apply the accreditation* Criteria *to their work with infants and toddlers.*

Because development is so individual, these statements do not define infants *and* toddlers *by chronological age. For the purpose of clarity, the infant statement is directed toward the care of non-walking children and the toddler statement addresses caring for children from the time they are walking until they are between 2½ and 3-years-old.*

Integrated Components of
APPROPRIATE and INAPPROPRIATE Practice for
INFANTS

Component	APPROPRIATE Practice	INAPPROPRIATE Practice
Interactions among adults and children	• Adults engage in many one-to-one, face-to-face interactions with infants. Adults talk in a pleasant, soothing voice, and use simple language and frequent eye contact.	• Infants are left for long periods in cribs, playpens, or seats without adult attention. Adults are harsh, shout, or use baby talk.
	• Infants are held and carried frequently to provide them with a wide variety of experiences. The adults talk to the infant before, during, and after moving the infant around.	• Infants are wordlessly moved about at the adult's convenience. Nothing is explained to infants.
	• Adults are especially attentive to infants during routines such as diaper changing, feeding, and changing clothes. The caregiver explains what will happen, what is happening, and what will happen next.	• Routines are swiftly accomplished without involving the infant. Little or no warm interactions take place during routines.
	• All interactions are characterized by gentle, supportive responses. Adults listen and respond to sounds that infants make, imitate them, and respect infants' sounds as the beginning of comunication.	• Adults are rough, harsh, or ignore the child's responses.

34

Component	APPROPRIATE Practice	INAPPROPRIATE Practice
	• Caregivers respond quickly to infants' cries or calls of distress, recognizing that crying and body movements are infants' only way to communicate. Responses are soothing and tender.	• Crying is ignored or responded to irregularly at the convenience of the adult. Crying is treated as a nuisance. Adults' responses neglect the infants' needs.
	• Playful interactions with babies are done in ways that are sensitive to the child's level of tolerance for physical movement, louder sounds, or other changes.	• Adults frighten, tease, or upset children with their unpredictable behaviors.
	• Children's play interests are respected. Adults observe the child's activity and comment, offer additional ideas for play, and encourage the child's engagement in the activity.	• Infants are interrupted, toys are whisked from their grasp, adults impose their own ideas or even play with toys themselves regardless of the child's interest.
	• The caregiver frequently talks with, sings to, and reads to infants. Language is a vital, lively form of communication with individuals.	• Infants are expected to entertain themselves or watch television. Language is used infrequently and vocabularies limited.
	• Infants and their parents are greeted warmly and with enthusiasm each morning. The caregiver holds the baby upon arrival and gradually helps the child become a part of the small group.	• Babies are placed on the floor or in a crib with no caregiver interaction. Caregivers receive children coldly and without individual attention.
	• Caregivers consistently respond to infants' needs for food and comfort thus enabling the infants to develop trust in the adults who care for them, so they find the world a secure place to be.	• Adults are unpredictable and/or unresponsive. They act as if children are a bother.
	• Caregivers adjust to infants' individual feeding and sleeping schedules. Their food preferences and eating styles are respected.	• Schedules are rigid and based on adults' rather than children's needs. Food is used for rewards (or denied as punishment).
	• Infants are praised for their accomplishments and helped to feel increasingly competent.	• Infants are criticized for what they cannot do or for their clumsy struggle to master a skill. They are made to feel inadequate and that they have no effect on others.
	• Teachers respect infants' curiosity about each other. At the same time, adults help ensure that children treat each other gently.	• Infants are not allowed to touch each other gently, or are forced to share or play together when they have no interest in doing so.
	• Adults model the type of interactions with others that they want children to develop.	• Adults are aggressive, shout, or exhibit a lack of coping behaviors under stress.
	• Adults frequently engage in games such as Peek-a-Boo and 5 Little Piggies with infants who are interested and responsive to the play.	• Games are imposed on children regardless of their interest. Play is seen as a time filler rather than a learning experience.

35

Component	APPROPRIATE Practice	INAPPROPRIATE Practice
Interactions among adults and children (*continued*)	• Diaper changing, feeding, and other routines are viewed as vital learning experiences for babies.	• Routines are dealt with superficially and indifferently.
	• Healthy, accepting attitudes about children's bodies and their functions are expressed.	• Infants are made to feel their bodies are not to be touched or admired, and that bodily functions are disgusting.
Environment	• The diapering, sleeping, feeding, and play areas are separate to ensure sanitation and provide quiet, restful areas.	• Areas are combined and are very noisy and distracting.
	• The environment contains both soft (pillows, padded walls) and hard (rocking chair, mirrors) elements.	• The environment is either sterile or cluttered, but lacks variety.
	• Babies find contrasts in color and design interesting, so bright colors are used to create distinct patterns.	• Rooms are sterile and bland.
	• Children have their own cribs, bedding, feeding utensils, clothing, diapers, pacifiers, and other special comforting objects. Infants' names are used to label every personal item.	• Infants share sleeping quarters in shifts, or otherwise do not have their own special supplies.
	• The area that is the focus of play changes periodically during the day from the floor, to strollers, to being carried, to rocking or swinging, and other variations to give infants different perspectives on people and places. Children are cared for both indoors and outdoors.	• Babies are confined to cribs, playpens, or the floor for long periods indoors. Time outdoors is viewed as too much bother, or is not done because of excuses about the weather.
	• Mirrors are placed where infants can observe themselves—on the wall next to the floor, next to the diapering area.	• Children never have a chance to see themselves.
	• Fresh air and healthy heat/humidity/ cooling conditions are maintained.	• Rooms are too hot or too cold.
	• The room is cheerful and decorated at children's eye level with pictures of people's faces, friendly animals, and other familiar objects. Pictures of children and their families are displayed.	• Areas are dingy and dark. Decorations are at adult eye level and are uninteresting. No family photos are displayed.
	• A variety of music is provided for enjoyment in listening/body movement/ singing.	• Music is used to distract or lull infants to sleep. Children hear only children's songs.
	• Space is arranged so children can enjoy moments of quiet play by themselves, so they have space to roll over, and so they can crawl toward interesting objects.	• Space is cramped and unsafe for children who are learning how to move their bodies.
	• Floors are covered by easy-to-clean carpet. Infants are barefoot whenever possible.	• Floor coverings are dirty or hard and cold. Infants must wear shoes.

Component	APPROPRIATE Practice	INAPPROPRIATE Practice
Equipment	• Toys are safe, washable, and too large for infants to swallow. They range from very simple to more complex.	• Toys are sharp, tiny, with chipping paint, or otherwise unsafe and not washable. Toys are too simple or too complex for the infants served.
	• Toys provided are responsive to the child's actions: bells, busy boards, balls, vinyl-covered pillows to climb on, large beads that snap together, nesting bowls, small blocks, shape sorters, music boxes, squeeze toys that squeak.	• Toys are battery-powered or wind up so the baby just watches. Toys lack a variety of texture, size, and shape.
	• Mobiles are designed to be seen from the child's viewpoint. They are removed when children can reach for and grasp them.	• Mobiles are out of infants' vision. They are positioned where children can reach them.
	• Toys are scaled to a size that enables infants to grasp, chew, and manipulate them (clutch balls, rattles, spoons, teethers, rubber dolls).	• Toys are too large to handle, or unsafe for children to chew on.
	• Toys are available on open shelves so children can make their own selections.	• Toys are dumped in a box or kept out of children's reach forcing them to depend on adults' selection.
	• Low climbing structures and steps are provided. Structures are well padded and safe for exploration.	• No provisions are made for children to climb, or structures are only safe for older, more mobile children.
	• Books are heavy cardboard with rounded edges. They have bright pictures of familiar objects.	• Books are not available, or are made of paper that tears easily. Books do not contain objects familiar or interesting to children. Faded colors or intricate drawings are used.
	• Pictorial materials depict a variety of ages and ethnic groups in a positive way.	• Pictures are limited to cartoon characters or stereotypes.
Health, safety, and nutrition	• Health and safety precautions are taken to limit the spread of infectious disease. Toys that are mouthed are replaced when a child has finished with them so they can be cleaned with a bleach solution.	• Toys are scattered on the floor and cleaned occasionally, not at all, or improperly. Bottles sit on the floor. Spills are ignored.
	• Written records are maintained for each child. Immunizations are current. Up-to-date emergency information is readily available.	• Written records are incomplete or outdated.
	• Staff are in good health and take precautions not to spread infection.	• Because of limited sick leave, staff come to work even when they are ill.
	• Children are always under adult supervision.	• Children are left unattended.
	• The environment is safe for children—electrical outlets are covered, no hazardous substances are within children's reach, no extension cords are exposed.	• Children are frequently told "no" to hazards that should be removed. Rocking chairs are placed in crawling areas.

Component	APPROPRIATE Practice	INAPPROPRIATE Practice
	• Children are dressed appropriately for the weather and type of play they engage in.	• Infants' clothing is too confining, uncomfortable, or difficult to manage. Infants are over- or under-dressed.
Health, Safety, and nutrition (*continued*)	• Adults wash their hands before and after each diaper change, before and after feeding each infant.	• Adults are too casual or inconsistent about handwashing.
	• Adults are aware of the symptoms of common illnesses, environmental hazards such as lead poisoning, and food or other allergies.	• Staff do not notice or ignore changes in children's normal behavior or do not know children well enough to detect unusual behavior.
	• Diaper changing areas are easily and routinely sanitized after each change.	• Several children are changed on the same surface without sanitizing it for each child.
	• Children are always held with their bodies at an angle when being fed from a bottle.	• Bottles are propped up for children or children are left lying down with a bottle.
	• Children who can sit up eat in groups of one or two with a caregiver to ensure adult assistance as needed. Finger foods are encouraged. Only healthy foods are fed. Eating is considered a sociable, happy time.	• Large groups of children are fed in sequence or left to their own devices. Cookies and other sugary foods are used as treats. Children are not allowed to mess with their food. Conversation is limited.
Staff-parent interactions	• Parents are viewed as the child's primary source of affection and care. Staff support parents and work with them to help them feel confident as parents.	• Staff feel in competition with parents. They avoid controversial issues rather than resolving them with parents.
	• Parents and staff talk daily to share pertinent information about the child.	• Staff rarely talk with parents except at planned conferences.
	• Staff help parents anticipate the child's next areas of development and prepare them to support the child.	• Staff fail to provide parents with information or insights to help them do what is best for their child.
Staff qualifications	• Staff enjoy working with infants and are warmly responsive to their needs. Staff have had training specifically related to infant development and caregiving. They know what skills and behaviors emerge during the first few months, and support children as they become increasingly competent and knowledgeable. Staff are competent in first aid.	• Staff view work with infants as a chore and as custodial in nature. Staff have little or no training specific to infant development. They have unrealistic expectations for this age group. They are unaware of what to look for that might signal problems in development.
Staffing	• The group size and ratio of adults to infants is limited to allow for one-to-one interaction, intimate knowledge of individual babies, and consistent caregiving. Babies need to relate to the same, very few people each day. A ratio of 1 adult to no more than 3 infants is best.	• Group size and staff-child ratio are too large to permit individual attention and constant supervision. Staffing patterns require infants to relate to more than 2 different adults during the caregiving day.

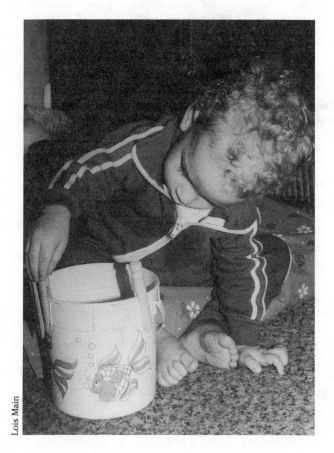

Lois Main

Subjects & Predicates

Adults must be especially careful to give toddlers many chances to figure things out for themselves, while remaining available to them if they ask for assistance.

When children direct their own play, they see themselves as competent people.

Integrated Components of
APPROPRIATE and INAPPROPRIATE Practice for
TODDLERS

Component	APPROPRIATE Practice	INAPPROPRIATE Practice
Interactions among adults and children	• Adults engage in many one-to-one, face-to-face conversations with toddlers. Adults let toddlers initiate language, and wait for a response, even from children whose language is limited. Adults label or name objects, describe events, and reflect feelings to help children learn new words. Adults simplify their language for toddlers who are just beginning to talk (instead of "It's time to wash our hands and have snack," the adult says, "Let's wash hands. Snacktime!" Then as children acquire their own words, adults expand on the toddler's language (for example, *Toddler*—"Mary sock." *Adult*—"Oh, that's Mary's missing sock and you found it.").	• Adults talk *at* toddlers and do not wait for a response. Adult voices dominate or adults do not speak to children because they think they are too young to respond. Adults either talk "baby talk" or use language that is too complex for toddlers to understand.
	• Adults are supportive of toddlers as they acquire skills. Adults watch to see what the child is trying to do and provide the necessary support to help the child accomplish the task, allowing children to do what they are capable of doing and assisting with tasks that are frustrating.	• Adults are impatient and intrusive. They expect too much or too little of toddlers. Because it is faster, adults do tasks for toddlers that children can do themselves. Or adults allow children to become frustrated by tasks they cannot do.
	• Adults respond quickly to toddlers' cries or calls for help, recognizing that toddlers have limited language with which to communicate their needs.	• Crying is ignored or responded to irregularly or at the adults' convenience.
	• Adults respect children's developing preferences for familiar objects, foods, and people. Adults permit children to keep their own favorite objects and provide limited options from which children may choose what they prefer to eat or wear. Children's preferences are seen as a healthy indication of a developing self-concept.	• Adults prohibit favored objects like blankets or toys or arbitrarily take them away or expect toddlers to share them with other children. Children are not given choices and preferences are not encouraged. Children are all expected to do the same thing.
	• Adults respect toddlers' desire to carry favored objects around with them, to move objects like household items from one place to another, and to roam around or sit and parallel play with toys and objects.	• Adults restrict objects to certain locations and do not tolerate hoarding, collecting, or carrying.

Component	APPROPRIATE Practice	INAPPROPRIATE Practice
Interactions among adults and children (*continued*)	• Adults patiently redirect toddlers to help guide children toward controlling their own impulses and behavior. When children fight over the same toy, the adult provides another like it or removes the toy. If neither of these strategies is effective, the adult may gently remove the toddler and redirect the child's attention by initiating play in another area. Adults only punish children for overtly dangerous behavior.	• Adults ignore disputes leading to a chaotic atmosphere or punish infractions harshly, frightening and humiliating children.
	• Adults recognize that constantly testing limits and expressing opposition to adults ("NO!") is part of developing a healthy sense of self as a separate, autonomous individual. Adults only say "No" when the prohibition relates to children's safety. Adults give positively worded directions ("Bang on the floor") not just restrictions ("Don't bang on the table").	• Adults are constantly saying "No!" to toddlers or becoming involved in power struggles over issues that do not relate to the child's health or well-being. Adults punish children for asserting themselves or saying "No."
	• Children are praised for their accomplishments and helped to feel increasingly competent and in control of themselves.	• Toddlers are criticized for what they cannot do or for their clumsy struggle to master a skill. Or adults foster dependency; children are overprotected and made to feel inadequate.
	• Children and their parents are greeted warmly and with enthusiasm each morning. The day begins with a great deal of adult-child contact. Adults help toddlers settle into the group by reading books or quietly playing with them.	• Children are received coldly and given no individual attention. Toddlers are expected to begin the day with free play and little adult supervision.
	• Adults model the type of interactions with others that they want children to develop. Adults recognize that most of the time when toddlers are aggressive, hurting or biting other children, it is because they lack skills to cope with frustrating situations such as wanting another child's toy. Adults model for toddlers the words to say ("Susan, I want the jack-in-the-box now") or redirect them to another activity.	• Adults are aggressive, shout, or exhibit a lack of coping behaviors under stress. Adult attempts to punish or control the aggressive toddler escalate the hostility.
Living and learning with toddlers (curriculum)	• Adults recognize that routine tasks of living like eating, toileting, and dressing are important opportunities to help children learn about their world and to regulate their own behavior.	• Routine times are chaotic because all children are expected to do the same thing at the same time.

Component	APPROPRIATE Practice	INAPPROPRIATE Practice
Living and learning with toddlers (curriculum) (*continued*)	• Adults play with toddlers reciprocally, modeling for toddlers how to play imaginatively with baby dolls and accessories. For example, adults and children play "tea party" where the adult pretends to drink from a cup and exclaims how good it tastes and then the toddler often models the adult.	• Adults do not play with toddlers because they feel silly or bored.
	• Adults support toddlers' play so that toddlers stay interested in an object or activity for longer periods of time and their play becomes more complex, moving from simple awareness and exploration of objects to more complicated play like pretending.	• Adults do not think that supporting children's play is important. They do not understand the value of play for learning or they feel silly playing with young children.
	• Toddlers' solitary and parallel play is respected. Adults provide several of the same popular toys for children to play with alone or near another child. Adults realize that having three or four of the same sought-after toy is more helpful than having one each of many different toys.	• Adults do not understand the value of solitary and parallel play and try to force children to play together. Adults arbitrarily expect children to share. Popular toys are not provided in duplicate and fought over constantly while other toys are seldom used.
	• Adults prepare the environment to allow for predictability and repetition, as well as events that can be expected and anticipated.	• Adults lose patience with doing many of the same things repeatedly and get bored by toddlers' needs to repeat tasks until they master them or feel secure in a predictable environment.
	• Adults frequently read to toddlers, individually on laps or in groups of two or three. Adults sing with toddlers, do fingerplays, act out simple stories like "The Three Bears" with children participating actively, or tell stories using a flannelboard or magnetic board, and allow children to manipulate and place figures on the boards.	• Adults impose "group time" on toddlers, forcing a large group to listen or watch an activity without opportunity for children to participate.
	• Toddlers are given appropriate art media such as large crayons, watercolor markers, and large paper. Adults expect toddlers to explore and manipulate art materials and do *not* expect them to produce a finished art product. Adults *never* use food for art because toddlers are developing self-regulatory skills and must learn to distinguish between food and other objects that are not to be eaten.	• Toddlers are "helped" by teachers to produce a product, follow the adult-made model, or color a coloring book or ditto sheet. Tactilely sensitive toddlers are required to fingerpaint or are given edible fingerpaint or playdough because they will probably put it in their mouths.

Component	APPROPRIATE Practice	INAPPROPRIATE Practice
Living and learning with toddlers (curriculum) (*continued*)	• Time schedules are flexible and smooth, dictated more by children's needs than by adults. There is a relatively predictable sequence to the day to help children feel secure.	• Activities are dictated by rigid adherence to time schedules or the lack of any time schedule makes the day unpredictable.
	• Children's schedules are respected with regard to eating and sleeping. Toddlers are provided snacks more frequently and in smaller portions than older children. For example, 2 morning snacks are offered at earlier hours than are usually provided for preschoolers. Liquids are provided frequently. Children's food preferences are respected.	• Schedules are rigid and based on adults' rather than children's needs. Food is used for rewards or withheld as punishment. Children are allowed to become fussy and cranky waiting for food that is served on a rigid schedule.
	• Diaper changing, toilet learning, eating, dressing, and other routines are viewed as vital learning experiences.	• Routines are dealt with superficially and indifferently.
	• Children learn to use the toilet through consistent, positive encouragement by adults. When toddlers reach an age where they feel confident and unafraid to sit a potty seat, adults invite them to use the potty, help them as needed, provide manageable clothing, and positively reinforce their behavior regardless of the outcome. Children are provided a toddler-appropriate potty seat and step-stool, if needed, in a well-lit, inviting, relatively private space. Children are taken to the toilet frequently and regularly in response to their own biological habits. Toddlers are never scolded or shamed about toileting or wet diapers/pants.	• Toilet learning is imposed on children to meet the adults' needs, whether children are ready or not. Children are made to sit on the potty for undue lengths of time and only reinforced contingent on urinating or defecating in the potty. Children are punished or shamed for toileting accidents.
	• Healthy, accepting attitudes about children's bodies and their functions are expressed.	• Children are made to feel their bodies are not to be to admired, and that bodily functions are disgusting.
	• Children have daily opportunities for exploratory activity outdoors, such as water and sand play and easel painting. Waterplay is available daily, requiring that adults dry clothes or provide clothing changes. Children have opportunities for supervised play in sand. Adults recognize that sand is a soft and absorbing medium ideally suited for toddler exploration. Well-supervised sand play is used to teach children to self-regulate what they can and cannot eat.	• Adults do not offer water and sand play because they are messy and require supervision, using as an excuse that children will get wet or will eat sand. Children's natural enjoyment of water play is frustrated so they play in toilets or at sinks whenever they can.

Component	APPROPRIATE Practice	INAPPROPRIATE Practice
Living and learning with toddlers (curriculum) (*continued*)	• Routines are planned as learning experiences to help children become skilled and independent. Meals and snacks include finger food or utensils that are easier for toddlers to use such as bowls, spoons, and graduated versions of drinking objects from bottles to cups. Dressing and undressing are seen as learning activities and children's attempts to dress themselves and put on shoes are supported and positively encouraged.	• Adults foster children's dependence by doing routine tasks for them that they could do for themselves. Children feel incompetent because the eating utensils are too difficult for them or clothes require adult assistance with tiny buttons or laces.
	• Food is ready before children are called to meals so they do not have to wait.	• Hungry toddlers become frustrated and cranky when they are set up to eat and then must wait to be served.
Environment	• The diapering/toileting, sleeping, feeding, and play areas are separate both for sanitation and to ensure quiet, restful areas.	• Areas are combined and very noisy and distracting.
	• The environment contains both soft (pillows, padded walls, carpeting) and hard (rocking chairs, mirrors) elements.	• The environment is dominated by hard surfaces because they are easier to keep clean.
	• The environment contains private spaces with room for no more than 2 children.	• The environment provides no private spaces.
	• Children have their own cribs or cots, bedding, feeding utensils, clothing, and other special comforting objects. Toddlers' names are used to label every personal item.	• Children share sleeping quarters in shifts, or otherwise do not have their own special supplies. Favored objects are not permitted.
	• Children have many opportunities for active, large muscle play both indoors and outdoors. The environment includes ramps and steps that are the correct size for children to practice newly acquired skills. Toddlers' outdoor play space is separate from that of older children. Outdoor play equipment for toddlers includes small climbing equipment that they can go around, in, and out of, and solitary play equipment requiring supervision such as swings and low slides.	• Toddlers' indoor space is cramped and unsafe for children who are just learning how to move their bodies and need to run more than walk. Toddlers share outdoor space and unsafe equipment designed for older children.
	• The room is cheerful and decorated at the children's eye level with pictures of faces of people, friendly animals, and other familiar objects. Pictures of children and their families are encouraged.	• Areas are dingy and dark. Decorations are at adult eye levels, or are too syrupy and cute. No evidence exists of personal involvement for families.

Component	APPROPRIATE Practice	INAPPROPRIATE Practice
Environment (*continued*)	• Sturdy picture books are provided. Pictures depict a variety of ages and ethnic groups in a positive way. • Toys are available on open shelves so children can make their own selections. Toys can be carried and moved about in the environment as children choose. • Climbing structures and steps are low, well-padded, and safe for exploration.	• Books are not available because they get torn or soiled. Pictures are cartoons or other stereotypes. • Toys are dumped in a box or kept away from children's reach so they are at the mercy of the adult's selection. Adults attempt to restrict the use of toys to certain areas, like housekeeping or blocks. • No provisions are made for children to climb, or structures are safe only for older, more mobile children.
Health, safety, and nutrition	• Health and safety precautions are taken to limit the spread of infectious disease. Toys that are mouthed are replaced when a child has finished with them so they can be cleaned with a bleach solution. • Written records are maintained for each child. Immunizations are current. Up-to-date emergency information is readily available. • Staff are in good health and take precautions not to spread infection. • Children are always under adult supervision. • The environment is safe for children—electrical outlets are covered, no hazardous substances are within children's reach, no extension cords are exposed. • Children are dressed appropriately for the weather and type of play they engage in. • Adults wash their hands before and after each diaper change, before and after assisting children with toileting, and before handling food. • Adults are aware of the symptoms of common illnesses, alert to changes in children's behavior that may signal illness or allergies. • Diaper changing areas are easily and routinely sanitized after each change.	• Toys are scattered on the floor and cleaned occasionally, not at all, or improperly. • Written records are incomplete or outdated. • Because of limited or no sick leave, staff come to work even when they are ill. • Children are left unattended. • Children are frequently told "no" to hazards that should be removed. • Toddlers' clothing is too confining, uncomfortable, or difficult to manage. • Adults are inconsistent or too casual about handwashing. • Staff do not notice or ignore changes in children's behavior or do not know children well enough to detect changes in normal patterns of behavior. • Several children are changed on the same surface.
Staff-parent interactions	• Parents are viewed as the child's primary source of affection and care. Staff support parents and work with them to help them feel confident as parents.	• Staff feel in competition with parents. They avoid controversial issues rather than resolving them with parents.

45

Component	APPROPRIATE Practice	INAPPROPRIATE Practice
Staff-parent interactions (*continued*)	• Parents and staff talk daily to share pertinent information about the child. There is an established system for keeping records of children's daily activity and health and reporting to parents.	• Staff rarely talk with parents except at planned conferences.
	• Staff help parents anticipate the child's next areas of development and prepare them to support the child.	• Staff fail to provide parents with information or insights to help them do what is best for their child.
Staff qualifications	• Staff enjoy working with toddlers, are warmly responsive to their needs, and demonstrate considerable patience in supporting children as they become increasingly competent and independent. Staff have training in child development and early education specific to the toddler age group. Staff are competent in first aid.	• Staff view work with toddlers as a chore and as custodial in nature. They push children to achieve and are impatient with their struggles, or they expect too little of toddlers. They are unaware of what to look for that might signal problems in development. Staff have no training in child development/early education or their training and experience are limited to working with older children.
Staffing	• The group size and ratio of adults to children is limited to allow for the intimate, interpersonal atmosphere, and high level of supervision toddlers require. Maximum group size is 12 with 1 adult for no more than 6 toddlers, preferably fewer. Staffing patterns limit the number of different adults toddlers relate to each day.	• Group size and staff-child ratio are too large to allow for individual attention and close supervision. Staff contain the chaos rather than respond to and support individual development. Staffing patterns require toddlers to relate to several different adults who do not know them well.

In a good program, adults respect children's choice to share only when the children are willing to do so.

Subjects & Predicates

PART 4

NAEYC Position Statement on Developmentally Appropriate Practice in Programs for 4- and 5-Year-Olds

Background information

In the mid 1980s, a great deal of public attention has focused on the quality of our nation's educational system. Early childhood education programs for 4- and 5-year-old children have become the focus of some controversy. Various issues are under debate, including the length of program day for this age group, the effect of various forms of sponsorship, and the nature of the curriculum.

Curriculum issues are of particular concern to early childhood educators in light of the increasingly widespread demand for use of inappropriate formal teaching techniques for young children, over-emphasis on achievement of narrowly defined academic skills, and increased reliance on psychometric tests to determine enrollment and retention in programs.

These trends are primarily the result of misconceptions about how young children learn (Elkind, 1986). In many cases, concerned adults, who want children to succeed, apply adult education standards to the curriculum for young children and pressure early childhood programs to demonstrate that children are "really learning." Many programs respond by emphasizing academic skill development with paper-and-pencil activities that are developmentally inappropriate for young children.

The National Association for the Education of Young Children (NAEYC), the nation's largest professional association of early childhood educators, believes that high quality, developmentally appropriate programs should be available for all 4- and 5-year-old children. NAEYC believes that quality is not determined by the length of the program day or by the sponsorship, although these factors can affect quality. NAEYC believes that a major determinant of the quality of an early childhood program is the degree to which the program is developmentally appropriate. This position statement describes both appropriate practices and inappropriate practices in early childhood programs. These beliefs about appropriate practice are supported by a growing body of both laboratory and clinical classroom research and theory. This statement is intended for use by teachers, parents, school administrators, policy makers, and others who provide educational programs for 4- and 5-year-olds.

Position Statement

How young children learn

Young children learn by doing. The work of Piaget (1950, 1972), Montessori (1964), Erikson (1950), and other child development theorists and researchers (Elkind, 1986; Kamii, 1985) has demonstrated that learning is a complex process that results from the interaction of children's own thinking and their experiences in the external world. Maturation is an important contributor to learning because it provides a framework from which children's learning proceeds. As children get older, they acquire new skills and experiences that facilitate the learning process. For example, as children grow physically, they are more able to manipulate and explore their own environment. Also, as children mature, they are more able to understand the point of view of other people.

47

Knowledge is not something that is given to children as though they were empty vessels to be filled. Children acquire knowledge about the physical and social worlds in which they live through playful interaction with objects and people. Children do not need to be forced to learn; they are motivated by their own desire to make sense of their world.

How to teach young children

How young children learn should determine how teachers of young children teach. The word *teach* tends to imply *telling* or *giving information.* But the correct way to teach young children is not to lecture or verbally instruct them. Teachers of young children are more like guides or facilitators (Forman & Kuschner, 1983; Lay-Dopyera & Dopyera, 1986; Piaget, 1972). They prepare the environment so that it provides stimulating, challenging materials and activities for children. Then, teachers closely observe to see what children understand and pose additional challenges to push their thinking further.

For children to fully understand and remember what they have learned, whether it is related to reading, mathematics, or other subject matter areas, the information must be meaningful to the child in context of the child's experience and development.

Children work individually or in small, informal groups most of the time.

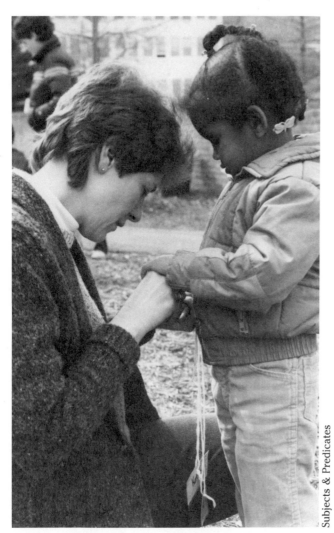

Interactions and activities are designed to develop children's self-esteem and positive feelings toward learning.

It is possible to drill children until they can correctly recite pieces of information such as the alphabet or the numerals from 1 to 20. However, children's responses to rote tasks do not reflect real understanding of the information. For children to understand fully and remember what they have learned, whether it is related to reading, mathematics, or other subject matter areas, the information must be meaningful to the child in context of the child's experience and development.

Learning information in meaningful context is not only essential for children's understanding and development of concepts, but is also important for stimulating motivation in children. If learning is relevant for children, they are more likely to persist with a task and to be motivated to learn more.

Developmentally appropriate practice for 4- and 5-year-olds

Developmentally appropriate teaching strategies are based on knowledge of how young children learn. Curriculum derives from many sources such as the knowledge base of various disciplines, society, culture, and parents' desires. The degree to which both teaching strategies and the curriculum are developmentally appropriate is a major determinant of program quality. Developmentally appropriate programs are both age appropriate and individually appropriate; that is, the program is designed for the age group served and implemented with attention to the needs and differences of the individual children enrolled.

Because people develop concepts from both positive and negative examples, the components of a program for 4- and 5-year-olds are described here both in terms of what is appropriate and what is *not* appropriate practice. These components overlap considerably and have been identified here for purposes of clarity only.

Outdoor activity is planned daily so children can develop large muscle skills, learn about outdoor environments, and express themselves freely and loudly.

Integrated Components of
APPROPRIATE and INAPPROPRIATE Practice for
4- AND 5-YEAR OLD CHILDREN

Component	APPROPRIATE Practice	INAPPROPRIATE Practice
Curriculum goals	• Experiences are provided that meet children's needs and stimulate learning in all developmental areas—physical, social, emotional, and intellectual.	• Experiences are narrowly focused on the child's intellectual development without recognition that all areas of a child's development are interrelated.
	• Each child is viewed as a unique person with an individual pattern and timing of growth and development. The curriculum and adults' interaction are responsive to individual differences in ability and interests. Different levels of ability, development, and learning styles are expected, accepted, and used to design appropriate activities.	• Children are evaluated only against a predetermined measure, such as a standardized group norm or adult standard of behavior. All are expected to perform the same tasks and achieve the same narrowly defined, easily measured skills.
	• Interactions and activities are designed to develop children's self-esteem and positive feelings toward learning.	• Children's worth is measured by how well they conform to rigid expectations and perform on standardized tests.
Teaching strategies	• Teachers prepare the environment for children to learn through active exploration and interaction with adults, other children, and materials.	• Teachers use highly structured, teacher-directed lessons almost exclusively.
	• Children select many of their own activities from among a variety of learning areas the teacher prepares, including dramatic play, blocks, science, math, games and puzzles, books, recordings, art, and music.	• The teacher directs all the activity, deciding what children will do and when. The teacher does most of the activity for the children, such as cutting shapes, performing steps in an experiment.
	• Children are expected to be physically and mentally active. Children choose from among activities the teacher has set up or the children spontaneously initiate.	• Children are expected to sit down, watch, be quiet, and listen, or do paper-and-pencil tasks for inappropriately long periods of time. A major portion of time is spent passively sitting, listening, and waiting.
	• Children work individually or in small, informal groups most of the time.	• Large group, teacher-directed instruction is used most of the time.
	• Children are provided concrete learning activities with materials and people relevant to their own life experiences.	• Workbooks, ditto sheets, flashcards, and other similarly structured abstract materials dominate the curriculum.

50

Component	APPROPRIATE Practice	INAPPROPRIATE Practice
Teaching strategies (*continued*)	• Teachers move among groups and individuals to facilitate children's involvement with materials and activities by asking questions, offering suggestions, or adding more complex materials or ideas to a situation.	• Teachers dominate the environment by talking to the whole group most of the time and telling children what to do.
	• Teachers accept that there is often more than one right answer. Teachers recognize that children learn from self-directed problem solving and experimentation.	• Children are expected to respond correctly with one right answer. Rote memorization and drill are emphasized.
Guidance of socioemotional development	• Teachers facilitate the development of self-control in children by using positive guidance techniques such as modeling and encouraging expected behavior, redirecting children to a more acceptable activity, and setting clear limits. Teachers' expectations match and respect children's developing capabilities.	• Teachers spend a great deal of time enforcing rules, punishing unacceptable behavior, demeaning children who misbehave, making children sit and be quiet, or refereeing disagreements.
	• Children are provided many opportunities to develop social skills such as cooperating, helping, negotiating, and talking with the person involved to solve interpersonal problems. Teachers facilitate the development of these positive social skills at all times.	• Children work individually at desks or tables most of the time or listen to teacher directions in the total group. Teachers intervene to resolve disputes or enforce classroom rules and schedules.
Language development and literacy	• Children are provided many opportunities to see how reading and writing are useful before they are instructed in letter names, sounds, and word identification. Basic skills develop when they are meaningful to children. An abundance of these types of activities is provided to develop language and literacy through meaningful experience: listening to and reading stories and poems; taking field trips; dictating stories; seeing classroom charts and other print in use; participating in dramatic play and other experiences requiring communication; talking informally with other children and adults; and experimenting with writing by drawing, copying, and inventing their own spelling.	• Reading and writing instruction stresses isolated skill development such as recognizing single letters, reciting the alphabet, singing the alphabet song, coloring within predefined lines, or being instructed in correct formation of letters on a printed line.

Component	APPROPRIATE Practice	INAPPROPRIATE Practice
Cognitive development	• Children develop understanding of concepts about themselves, others, and the world around them through observation, interacting with people and real objects, and seeking solutions to concrete problems. Learnings about math, science, social studies, health, and other content areas are all integrated through meaningful activities such as those when children build with blocks; measure sand, water, or ingredients for cooking; observe changes in the environment; work with wood and tools; sort objects for a purpose; explore animals, plants, water, wheels and gears; sing and listen to music from various cultures; and draw, paint, and work with clay. Routines are followed that help children keep themselves healthy and safe.	• Instruction stresses isolated skill development through memorization and rote, such as counting, circling an item on a worksheet, memorizing facts, watching demonstrations, drilling with flashcards, or looking at maps. Children's cognitive development is seen as fragmented in content areas such as math, science, or social studies, and times are set aside to concentrate on each area.
Physical development	• Children have daily opportunities to use large muscles, including running, jumping, and balancing. Outdoor activity is planned daily so children can develop large muscle skills, learn about outdoor environments, and express themselves freely and loudly. • Children have daily opportunities to develop small muscles skills through play activities such as pegboards, puzzles, painting, cutting, and other similar activities.	• Opportunity for large muscle activity is limited. Outdoor time is limited because it is viewed as interfering with instructional time or, if provided, is viewed as recess (a way to get children to use up excess energy), rather than an integral part of children's learning environment. • Small motor activity is limited to writing with pencils, or coloring predrawn forms, or similar structured lessons.
Aesthetic development	• Children have daily opportunities for aesthetic expression and appreciation through art and music. Children experiment and enjoy various forms of music. A variety of art media are available for creative expression, such as easel and finger painting and clay.	• Art and music are provided only when time permits. Art consists of coloring predrawn forms, copying an adult-made model of a product, or following other adult-prescribed directions.
Motivation	• Children's natural curiosity and desire to make sense of their world are used to motivate them to become involved in learning activities.	• Children are required to participate in all activities to obtain the teacher's approval, to obtain extrinsic rewards like stickers or privileges, or to avoid punishment.

Component	APPROPRIATE Practice	INAPPROPRIATE Practice
Parent-teacher relations	• Teachers work in partnership with parents, communicating regularly to build mutual understanding and greater consistency for children.	• Teachers communicate with parents only about problems or conflicts. Parents view teachers as experts and feel isolated from their child's experiences.
Assessment of children	• Decisions that have a major impact on children (such as enrollment, retention, assignment to remedial classes) are based primarily on information obtained from observations by teachers and parents, not on the basis of a single test score. Developmental assessment of children's progress and achievement is used to plan curriculum, identify children with special needs, communicate with parents, and evaluate the program's effectiveness.	• Psychometric tests are used as the sole criterion to prohibit entrance to the program or to recommend that children be retained or placed in remedial classrooms.
Program entry	• In public schools, there is a place for every child of legal entry age, regardless of the developmental level of the child. No public school program should deny access to children on the basis of results of screening or other arbitrary determinations of the child's lack of readiness. The educational system adjusts to the developmental needs and levels of the children it serves; children are not expected to adapt to an inappropriate system.	• Eligible-age children are denied entry to kindergarten or retained in kindergarten because they are judged not ready on the basis of inappropriate and inflexible expectations.
Teacher qualifications	• Teachers are qualified to work with 4- and 5-year-olds through college-level preparation in Early Childhood Education or Child Development and supervised experience with this age group.	• Teachers with no specialized training or supervised experience working with 4- and 5-year-olds are viewed as qualified because they are state certified, regardless of the level of certification.
Staffing	• The group size and ratio of teachers to children is limited to enable individualized and age-appropriate programming. Four- and 5-year-olds are in groups of no more than 20 children with 2 adults.	• Because older children can function reasonably well in large groups, it is assumed that group size and number of adults can be the same for 4- and 5-year-olds as for elementary grades.

53

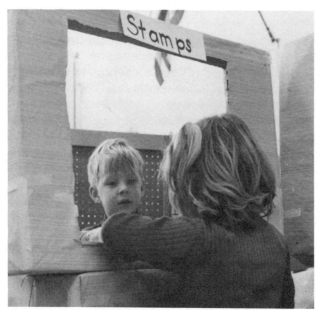

Children are provided many opportunities to see how reading and writing are useful before they are instructed in letter names, sounds, and word identification.

Joann Bush

Bibliography

These references include both laboratory and clinical classroom research to document the broad-based literature that forms the foundation for sound practice in early childhood education.

Related position statements

International Reading Association. (1985). *Literacy and pre-first grade.* Newark, DE: International Reading Association.

NAEYC. (1984). *Accreditation criteria and procedures of the National Academy of Early Childhood Programs.* Washington, DC: NAEYC.

NAEYC. (1986). *Position statement on developmentally appropriate practice in early childhood programs serving children from birth through age 8.*

Nebraska State Board of Education. (1984). *Position statement on kindergarten.* Lincoln, NE: Nebraska State Department of Education.

Southern Association on Children Under Six. (1984, July). A statement on developmentally appropriate educational experiences for kindergarten. *Dimensions, 12*(4), 25.

Southern Association on Children Under Six. (1986). *Position statement on quality four-year-old programs in public schools. Dimensions, 14*(3), 29.

Southern Association on Children Under Six. (1986). *Position statement on quality child care. Dimensions, 14*(4), p. 28.

State Department of Education, Columbia, South Carolina. (1983, rev. ed.). *Early childhood education in South Carolina. Learning experiences for 3-, 4-, and 5-year-old children.*

Texas Association for the Education of Young Children. (no date). *Developmentally appropriate kindergarten reading programs: A position statement.*

Developmentally appropriate practices and curriculum goals

Biber, B. (1984). *Early education and psychological development.* New Haven: Yale University Press.

Elkind, D. (1986, May). Formal education and early childhood education: An essential difference. *Phi Delta Kappan,* 631–636.

Erikson, E. (1950). *Childhood and society.* New York: Norton.

Kohlberg, L., & Mayer, R. (1972). Development as the arm of education. *Harvard Educational Review, 42,* 449–496.

Montessori, M. (1964). *The Montessori method.* Cambridge, MA: Robert Bentley.

Piaget, J. (1950). *The psychology of intelligence.* London: Routledge & Kegan Paul.

Piaget, J. (1952). *The origins of intelligence in children.* (M. Cook, Trans.) New York: Norton. (Original work published 1936)

Spodek, B. (1985). *Teaching in the early years* (3rd ed.). Englewood Cliffs, NJ: Prentice-Hall.

Weber, E. (1984). *Ideas influencing early childhood education: A theoretical analysis.* New York: Teachers College Press, Columbia University.

Teaching strategies

Fein, G. (1979). Play and the acquisition of symbols. In L. Katz (Ed.), *Current topics in early childhood education, Vol. 2.* Norwood, NJ: Ablex.

Fein, G., & Rivkin, M. (Eds.). (1986). *The young child at play: Reviews of research* (Vol. 4). Washington, DC: NAEYC.

Fromberg, D. (1986). Play. In C. Seefeldt (Ed.), *Early childhood curriculum: A review of current research.* New York: Teachers College Press, Columbia University.

Forman, G., & Kuschner, D. (1983). *The child's construction of knowledge: Piaget for teaching children.* Washington, DC: NAEYC.

Herron, R., & Sutton-Smith, B. (1974). *Child's play.* New York: Wiley.

Kamii, C. (1985). Leading primary education toward excellence: Beyond worksheets and drill. *Young Children, 40*(6), 3–9.

Languis, M., Sanders, T., & Tipps, S. (1980). *Brain and learning: Directions in early childhood education.* Washington, DC: NAEYC.

Lay-Dopyera, M., & Dopyera, J. (1986). Strategies for teaching. In C. Seefeldt (Ed.), *Early childhood curriculum: A review of current research.* New York: Teachers College Press, Columbia University.

Piaget, J. (1972). *Science of education and the psychology of the child* (rev. ed.). New York: Viking. (Original work published 1965)

Souweine, J.K., Crimmins, S., & Mazel, C. (1981). *Mainstreaming: Ideas for teaching young children.* Washington, DC: NAEYC.

Sponseller, D. (1982). Play and early education. In B. Spodek (Ed.), *Handbook of research in early childhood education.* New York: Free Press.

Guidance of socioemotional development

Asher, S. R., Renshaw, P. D., & Hymel, S. (1982). Peer relations and the development of social skills. In S. G. Moore & C. R. Cooper (Eds.), *The young child: Reviews of research* (Vol. 3, pp. 137–158). Washington, DC: NAEYC.

Erikson, E. (1950). *Childhood and society.* New York: Norton.

Honig, A. S. (1985). Research in review. Compliance, control, and discipline (Parts 1 & 2). *Young Children, 40*(2), 50–58; *40*(3), 47–52.

Moore, S. (1982). Prosocial behavior in the early years: Parent and peer influences. In B. Spodek (Ed.), *Handbook of research in early childhood education.* New York: Free Press.

Read, K.H., Gardner, P., & Mahler, B. (1986). *Early childhood programs: A laboratory for human relationships* (8th ed.). New York: Holt, Rinehart & Winston.

Rubin, K., & Everett, B. (1982). Social perspective-taking in young children. In S. G. Moore & C. R. Cooper (Eds.), *The young child: Reviews of research* (Vol. 3, pp. 97–114). Washington, DC: NAEYC.

Stone, J. (1978). *A guide to discipline* (rev. ed.). Washington, DC: NAEYC.

Language development and literacy

Cazden, C. (Ed.). (1981). *Language in early childhood education* (rev. ed.). Washington, DC: NAEYC.

Ferreiro, E., & Teberosky, A. (1982). *Literacy before schooling.* Exeter, NH: Heinemann.

Genishi, C. (1986). Acquiring language and communicative competence. In C. Seefeldt (Ed.), *Early childhood curriculum: A review of current research.* New York: Teachers College Press, Columbia University.

Schachter, F. F., & Strage, A. A. (1982). Adults' talk and children's language development. In S. G. Moore & C. R. Cooper (Eds.), *The young child: Reviews of research* (Vol. 3, pp. 79–96). Washington, DC: NAEYC.

Schickedanz, J. (1986). *More than the ABCs: The early stages of reading and writing.* Washington, DC: NAEYC.

Smith, F. (1982). *Understanding reading.* New York: Holt, Rinehart & Winston.

Willert, M., & Kamii, C. (1985). Reading in kindergarten: Direct versus indirect teaching. *Young Children, 40*(4), 3–9.

Cognitive development

Forman, G., & Kaden, M. (1986). Research on science education in young children. In C. Seefeldt (Ed.), *Early childhood curriculum: A review of current research.* New York: Teachers College Press, Columbia University.

Goffin, S., & Tull, C. (1985). Problem solving: Encouraging active learning. *Young Children, 40*(3), 28–32.

Kamii, C. (1982). *Number in preschool and kindergarten.* Washington, DC: NAEYC.

Hawkins, D. (1970). Messing about in science. *ESS Reader.* Newton, MA: Education Development Center.

Hirsch, E. (Ed.). (1984). *The block book.* Washington, DC: NAEYC.

Holt, B. (1979). *Science with young children.* Washington, DC: NAEYC.

Sackoff, E., & Hart, R. (1984, Summer). Toys: Research and applications. *Children's Environments Quarterly, 1–2.*

Wellman, H. M. (1982). The foundations of knowledge: Concept development in the young child. In S. G. Moore & C. R. Cooper (Eds.), *The young child: Reviews of research* (Vol. 3, pp. 115–134). Washington, DC: NAEYC.

Physical development

Cratty, B. (1982). Motor development in early childhood: Critical issues for researchers in the 1980's. In B. Spodek (Ed.), *Handbook of research in early childhood education.* New York: Free Press.

Curtis, S. (1986). New views on movement development and implications for curriculum in early childhood education. In C. Seefeldt(Ed.), *Early childhood curriculum: A review of current research.* New York: Teachers College Press, Columbia University.

Aesthetic development

Davidson, L. (1985). Preschool children's tonal knowledge: Antecedents of scale. In J. Boswell (Ed.), *The young child and music: Contemporary principles in child development and music education. Proceedings of the Music in Early Childhood Conference* (pp. 25–40). Reston, VA: Music Educators National Conference.

Evans, E. D. (1984). Children's aesthetics. In L. G. Katz (Ed.), *Current topics in early childhood education* (Vol. 5, pp. 73–104). Norwood, NJ: Ablex.

Gilbert, J. P. (1981). Motoric music skill development in young children: A longitudinal investigation. *Psychology of Music, 9*(1), 21–24.

Greenberg, M. (1976). Music in early childhood education: A survey with recommendations. *Council for Research in Music Education, 45,* 1–20.

Lasky, L., & Mukerji, R. (1980). *Art: Basic for young children.* Washington, DC: NAEYC.

McDonald, D. T. (1979). *Music in our lives: The early years.* Washington, DC: NAEYC.

Seefeldt, C. (1986). The visual arts. In C. Seefeldt (Ed.), *The early childhood curriculum: A review of current research.* New York: Teachers College Press, Columbia University.

Smith, N. (1983). *Experience and art: Teaching children to paint.* New York: Teachers College Press, Columbia University.

Motivation

Elkind, D. (1986). Formal education and early childhood education: An essential difference. *Phi Delta Kappan,* 631–636.

Gottfried, A. (1983). Intrinsic motivation in young children. *Young Children, 39*(1), 64–73.

Parent-teacher relations

Croft, D. J. (1979). *Parents and teachers: A resource book for home, school, and community relations.* Belmont, CA: Wadsworth.

Gazda, G. M. (1973). *Human relations development: A manual for educators.* Boston: Allyn & Bacon.

Honig, A. (1982). Parent involvement in early childhood education. In B. Spodek (Ed.), *Handbook of research in early childhood education.* New York: Free Press.

Katz, L. (1980). Mothering and teaching: Some significant distinctions. In L. Katz (Ed.), *Current topics in early childhood education* (Vol. 3, pp. 47–64). Norwood, NJ: Ablex.

Lightfoot, S. (1978). *Worlds apart: Relationships between families and schools.* New York: Basic.

Assessment of children

Cohen, D. H., Stern, V., & Balaban, N. (1983). *Observing and recording the behavior of young children* (3rd ed.). New York: Teachers College Press, Columbia University.

Goodman, W., & Goodman, L. (1982). Measuring young children. In B. Spodek (Ed.), *Handbook of research in early childhood education.* New York: Free Press.

Meisels, S. (1985). *Developmental screening in early childhood.* Washington, DC: NAEYC.

Standards for educational and psychological testing. (1985). Washington, DC: American Psychological Association, American Educational Research Association, and National Council on Measurement in Education.

Teacher qualifications and staffing

Almy, M. (1982). Day care and early childhood education. In E. Zigler & E. Gordon (Eds.), *Daycare: Scientific and social policy issues* (pp. 476–495). Boston: Auburn House.

Feeney, S., & Chun, R. (1985). Research in review. Effective teachers of young children. *Young Children, 41*(1), 47–52.

NAEYC. (1982). *Early childhood teacher education guidelines for four- and five-year programs.* Washington, DC: NAEYC.

Ruopp, R., Travers, J., Glantz, F., & Coelen, C. (1979). *Children at the center. Final report of the National Day Care Study, Vol. 1.* Cambridge, MA: Abt Associates.

Where Do We Go From Here?

This book would not be complete without addressing the question, "Where do we go from here?" Definitions are only valuable to the extent that they are used to clarify information and alleviate misunderstanding. When terminology is critical to a particular occupation or field of endeavor, it is equally critical that all practitioners agree on the definitions of important terms and use those terms similarly. In the field of early childhood education, one of the most important phrases in our professional jargon is *developmentally appropriate*. It is a key phrase that we use to communicate among ourselves and must begin to use with those outside our profession. For our communications to be understood, we must share the same meaning of the phrase. This book is a tool for early childhood professionals. Here are some ways this book can be used to advocate both within and outside the profession for developmentally appropriate programs for young children.

Advocating Within the Profession

Teachers, Directors, Teacher Trainers, Researchers

- Carefully read these positions and incorporate the terminology and definitions into your vocabulary.
- Compare your own practices to the practices described in this book.
- Refer to these definitions when talking to parents about what you do in your classroom. Use this book to justify appropriate practices when parents or others pressure you to push children in inappropriate ways.
- Establish networks and support groups with other teachers and/or directors in your community who strive to operate developmentally appropriate programs.
- Demonstrate that you operate a model program by working toward accreditation by NAEYC's National Academy of Early Childhood Programs.

- Use these definitions as a basic text when preparing new teachers to enter the field. An understanding of developmental appropriateness is the foundation for all future learning and practice in early childhood education.
- Use these examples and descriptions when conducting in-service training.
- Conduct research on the long-term effects on children of appropriate and inappropriate practices.

Advocating Outside the Profession

Parents, Policy Makers, Legislators, School Administrators

- Talk to parents about how you provide developmentally appropriate care and education for their children; describe what you do and why you do it.
- Quote from this book in newsletters to parents or use this book as a resource for a parent meeting.
- Use *Week of the Young Child* or other public forums to educate parents and the general public about appropriate teaching practices.
- Write to and meet with policy makers and legislators about the need to provide adequate resources and standards for developmentally appropriate programs. Quote from and reference this book to substantiate your position.
- Write to and meet with state department of education administrators and other program administrators about the importance of providing developmentally appropriate programs and the resources they require.
- Write to corporations or businesses about the products they sell or the programs they produce for children. Congratulate them when their product is developmentally appropriate or inform and educate them if their product is inappropriate for young children.

Elaine M. Ward

Teachers prepare the environment for children to learn through active exploration and interaction with adults, other children, and materials.

Children select many of their own activities from among a variety of learning areas the teacher prepares, including dramatic play, blocks, science, math, games and puzzles, books, recordings, art, and music.

Subjects & Predicates

Children are provided many opportunities to develop social skills such as cooperating, helping, negotiating, and talking with the person involved to solve interpersonal problems.

Paul M. Schrock Photos

Index